RACISM IN THE SOUTH…

IN MY TIME

THE EDUCATION OF A SOUTHERN GENTLEMAN

GEORGE E. DEVITT

A WHITE MAN'S JOURNEY OUT OF THE BONDS OF RACISM

RACISM IN THE SOUTH...

IN MY TIME

THE EDUCATION OF A SOUTHERN GENTLEMAN

GEORGE E. DEVITT

A WHITE MAN'S JOURNEY OUT OF THE BONDS OF RACISM

To Sharon, who educated me.

With love.

With understanding.

And with grace.

Accepting me without judgment.

Despite my ignorance.

Table of Contents

Foreword   9

Chapter 1: From the North to the South   35

Chapter 2: "Whuppins" Were   45
Commonplace

Chapter 3: Athletics: The Great Race Equalizer   51

Chapter 4: Dillon, South Carolina; My   65
Grandmother, and A Wage of $7 a Day

Chapter 5: Holley, Florida and a Dream Home   75

Chapter 6: An Uncomfortable   92
Confession

Chapter 7: Off to College   97

Chapter 8: Good Fortune   113

Chapter 9: Proud Marines: Into the Hotspots   124

Chapter 10: IBM: A New Brother and a   139
New Sister; Sharon Takes a Husband

Chapter 11: A Seminal Event; Finally,   154
an Admission

Chapter 12: My Continuing Education   165

About the Author   168

Afterword   173

Foreword

As with most boys, my father had a profound impact upon my life in many ways.

He was a career Marine who served in the Korean Conflict and the Vietnam War. He was born in the southeastern portion of Massachusetts which is home to Fall River and New Bedford. Once a successful whaling community, it had fallen on hard times during his childhood. At one point, Fall River was actually the largest textile manufacturing city in the United States, which was obviously a source of great pride to this tight-knit community. Technically, the area is considered part of the Providence (Rhode Island) metropolitan area. As with many other parts of Massachusetts which are home to large immigrant communities, the Fall River/New Bedford area hosts the largest community of Portuguese-Americans in the country.

My inclusion in this book of a significant amount of detail about my father – and my relationship with him – is threefold: one, because he did have a significant impact on me and my life; two, because of how his views about race and racism affected me; and lastly – something which I have never disclosed until I undertook the development of this book – because, like many, I suffer my fair share of dysfunctions. Most of these I attribute to my father and the manner in which he treated me during my childhood.   The reader needn't be concerned, though, that I am going to undertake a "deep dive" into the psycho-babble diagnosis *du jour* for which, it seems, almost everyone I know is being treated with the latest and greatest medication to cope with the natural ups and downs of life.

My father was from the generation which resisted taking prescription medications, or, as it often seemed, even visiting a physician on a routine basis. I remember an occasion as a ten-year old when I was visiting a doctor with my mother and she showed me my own medical records chart next to that of my father. Mine was probably an inch thick. His had only a handful of pages in it. I was 10. He was approaching 40.

I don't recall my father ever using derogatory language about blacks or any other race. I always assumed that this was either because he was brought up in the north, or because his military service included his living and working – often in close quarters – with other Marines of different skin colors. Of course, in a combat environment, Marines depend upon their co-combatants for their lives. A mistake by another Marine on whom one depends during a combat exercise -- could result in a brother-in-arms being killed.

While we never discussed race, I always assumed that he didn't harbor ill will toward any racial group.

I would later learn that this wasn't entirely true. To this day, I don't know if my understanding was wrong because of inaccurate assumptions by me or because he had changed his views about race as he grew older.

I was born in Wilmington, North Carolina, but only because my father was stationed at MCB Camp Lejeune at the time of my birth. The oldest of five children, I have four sisters. Their birthplaces follow the path of my father's postings up and down America's east coast.

My father was often gone for extended periods and stationed in places which were considered hostile to families, such as Cuba, Korea or Vietnam. Unlike many of my friends who grew up in military families and had the opportunity to experience life at United States bases in Germany, Japan and other foreign countries, the nature of my father's postings didn't allow for this. As a result, my mother was a "single parent" for much of my life. When my father was posted in the United States, the family lived where he was stationed: Glens Falls, New York, Springfield, Massachusetts, Dillon, South Carolina, as well as other, less memorable locations.

Essentially, though, I grew up in the heart of the south - in the panhandle of Florida. However, my somewhat unique perspectives regarding race are complex and cannot simply be dismissed by attributing them to the locale of my upbringing.

My father served for almost 22 years in the Marines, and our family moved often until his retirement. While my father was on active duty, the longest single period of time spent in one place was the period between my second-grade and seventh-grade years, which were spent in Springfield, Massachusetts. Springfield is a working-class town in western Massachusetts which is not particularly noteworthy for much – except that it is the home of the NBA's Basketball Hall of Fame, and because the city has been home to the game-maker, the Milton-Bradley Company for well over 100 years.

These five years spent in Springfield may have had as much of an impact, and perhaps an even greater impact, in shaping my beliefs and my "world view" (to the extent that a 4th – grader can have a "world view!") as any other period in my life.

Our family lived in an integrated neighborhood in Springfield, and my best friend was a black boy, Barry, who lived three doors down from our house. Curiously, I don't recall much attention being given to race or racism, with the exception of news stories in the print and broadcast media describing in great detail the events which were occurring in the South during this period of desegregation and forced school bussing. It was, after all, the mid-1960's.

My own recollection of Civil War history was very straightforward: The South supported slavery. Slavery was obviously wrong. The North went to war with the South to end the practice of slavery and defeated the Confederates. Period. Not much more was part of my education regarding this chapter of our nation's history.

It was in the middle of my 7th grade school year that my father retired from the Marine Corps. Or more accurately, he was *forced* to retire.

Upon his retirement, our family moved to Florida and settled in Florida's panhandle.

Florida is a unique state in many ways. At a minimum, it's really two states: northern Florida, including the panhandle, and the rest of the state. To this day,

Northern Florida remains much more like Alabama, Georgia and Mississippi with respect to its customs, mores, culture and views about race. Comparing the Florida Panhandle to Key West or to Miami or to Tampa or to Orlando is akin to comparing Los Angeles to Birmingham.

Our family settled in Santa Rosa County on a pristine island (Santa Rosa Island) which was home to Navarre Beach.

Navarre Beach is located in the southern-most part of Santa Rosa County. The nearest high school was in Milton, which was then and remains the County Seat. Milton is 28 miles north of Navarre Beach, and yet getting to Milton from Navarre Beach on the public school buses provided by the county, involved the Devitt children taking three separate buses in each direction. My sisters and I were the first ones to get on the bus – at about 5:45AM – and the last ones to get off of the bus – at about 5:00PM.

It was on the second bus ride when I observed something which I found curious. There was one particular bus stop made by the second of the three buses at which virtually every black student going to East Milton Elementary School, Hobbs Middle School or Milton High School boarded. At the dozens of other stops made by *three different buses*, not one black student boarded; it was only at this one bus stop. Beyond being merely curious, I became increasingly more knowledgeable and aware of a concept which had heretofore been foreign to me: that of segregation.

My remembrance is that my sisters and I were "color blind" when we lived in Springfield. It never occurred to me that blacks were any different from whites. I recall asking my best friend, Barry – a black boy – if the color of his urine was different from mine. Other than this one particular childhood curiosity, I have no recollection of even a passing thought that there might be differences between blacks and whites.

In addition to my curiosity about the single bus stop at which the black students all boarded, the other thing I found curious after moving to the South was the difference in views between people in my new home and those whom I'd left behind regarding the Civil War. My study of Civil War history while attending school in Massachusetts was, as I noted previously, simple and straightforward. But in my new home in Florida's Panhandle, I saw trucks with Confederate Flags on their bumpers. There were other bumper stickers with the Confederate Flag and text saying, "Hell No, I Won't Forget." I never spoke to any of my new friends about this, but recall finding it, too, curious. And a bit disturbing. My views were not shaped by any particularly exceptional knowledge that I may have had regarding the Civil Rights Movement or the struggles which blacks faced in the South. My curiosity and the degree to which I found these things *different* in the South were purely based on my observations of peers who lived near my old home and those residing near my new one.

A shy student, I didn't make friends easily. Initially, I didn't have any reason to believe there were differences between black people in Florida and black people in Massachusetts. But these views didn't last for very long, as eventually I did come to believe that blacks in my new home *were* different from those I'd left behind in Springfield. It was this conclusion, disturbing and controversial though it was, that provided the essence of my evolving views regarding race and is the foundation for this book.

Both of my parents were chronic alcoholics during my childhood (although, to their credit, both eventually did stop drinking). My father was at times violent when drinking or when drunk. On more than one occasion I recall being on the unpleasant end of my father's combat boot or his clenched fist. To be honest, much of this history and any memory of these events have been lost. It is fortunate – or unfortunate – that my mother and younger sisters had memories better than my own and did recall these events.

While stationed in Springfield, Massachusetts at a recruiting office, my father was involved in several incidents of "Driving While Intoxicated," or as it's known in Massachusetts, "DWI." I remember one incident in great detail because my father had broken all of his ribs, several other bones and his jaw, which was wired shut.

When he finally was discharged from the hospital, he could only eat (or drink) through a straw at home. With the benefit of hindsight, it's remarkable that he survived the accident, which is a testament to the man's "survivability."

In an agreement between local law enforcement and the Marine Corps, the DWI charges against my father were dropped on the condition that he be sent to Vietnam. Not unexpectedly, as soon as he recovered from the injuries suffered in the automobile accident, he was on an airplane destined for Saigon.

With no disrespect to any service member who served in Vietnam, it was clear to me that the Marines were thrust into the combat "hot spots." My father was sent to what was known at the time as "The De-Militarized Zone," or the "DMZ." Even as a young man, the irony of this oxymoron was not lost on me.

After less than a year into his tour in Vietnam, I remember my mother pointing to a newspaper article about a Marine Corps company which had been almost completely annihilated, and her saying to me – with considerable conviction – "I think this included your father." To this day, I don't know what instincts led her to that conclusion, but she was right.

We rarely heard from our father when he was in Vietnam because of how deep he was engaged in combat zones. But within weeks of the newspaper article appearing and my mother's stating her belief that the combat included my father, we received a postcard in the mail.

The postcard was from my father, and was sent from a hospital ship. It said, quite simply: "...Well, the war's over. At least for me..." We didn't know any more than what was included on this cryptic note, and had no idea of when he'd arrive back home, the extent of his injuries or the circumstances which resulted in his being injured.

My father never told "war stories" as many veterans do. In fact, the only stories he ever told about his military experiences had a humorous bent or evidenced his disregard for authority in one way or another.   A favorite was when he was stationed in Guantanamo Bay, Cuba, known commonly as "Gitmo."   While at Gitmo, very late one night he went to the end of a pier with a floodlight. Shining the floodlight into the warm waters of the Caribbean Sea, the light attracted insects, which in turn attracted small fish, which of course attracted even larger fish. When he had determined that a sufficient number of larger fish had "schooled" under the light, he tossed a hand grenade into the water. After it exploded, all of the now-dead fish floated to the surface, after which my father used a net to scoop up dozens of snook, trout and other fish.

Of course, the story didn't end there. His antics resulted in disciplinary action and the loss of one stripe or "rank." But I'm sure that to my father, it was well worth it. It was probably well worth it just for the story-telling value the event held!

My father enlisted in the Marines when he was seventeen. During his almost 22-year career, he was offered opportunities to move into the ranks of the officer corps. But accepting such a "promotion" would have resulted in a short-term cut in pay, although in the long run it would have been far more financially beneficial. Every time he was offered a promotion to become an officer, he declined.

The enlisted ranks of the Marine Corps (and the other services) are on a scale ranging from E-1 to E-9. Under ordinary circumstances, almost anyone who served for almost 22 years and fought in two wars would have retired as an E-9, which in the Marines would be a Sergeant Major or a Master Gunnery Sergeant. But, due to my father's antic-filled career, he retired as an E-7, or a Gunnery Sergeant. Typically, this rank is achieved after only 12 years or so in the Marines. This was significant because the retirement pay awarded to anyone serving twenty years or more in the military is a function of the individual's active-duty salary and the number of years of service. Thus, he paid for his "antics" with a reduced retirement income, which he received for far longer than he received his active duty income.

When my father returned from Vietnam, his injuries were so severe that he could no longer serve and he was forced to retire. So, at 39, I had a father who was retired. Our family had been living in Springfield, Massachusetts, for about five years. And in the benevolence of the military, its view is that the military family shouldn't be forced to live for the remainder of their lives in the city in which the service member happened to be stationed at the time of his or her retirement. So the military's policy is (or was) to pay for one more relocation to a destination of the service member's choosing (within reason). To a family living in Massachusetts, which was the state of my father's birth, and putting up with blizzards and harsh winters, the notion of moving to Florida seemed to have an almost fantasy-like allure. Without any research, our family sold our home, loaded up our station wagon, and drove to Florida.

The Florida Panhandle became our home for two reasons: 1) my father was, frankly, tired of driving, and 2) our family would benefit from the dozens of military bases and other posts which blanket the Panhandle. This would allow our family to take advantage of a vast array of military benefits: free medical care, shopping at subsidized grocery stores and department stores on-base – basically all of the benefits that an active-duty family enjoyed.

For years, that Congressional District was represented by The Honorable Robert L. F. Sykes. Bob Sykes was Chairman of a rather arcane committee which was a subcommittee of a subcommittee of the House Armed Services Committee. It was the House Subcommittee on Military Construction. And Sykes used his position to benefit his district in ways too significant to enumerate. Within Sykes' district were the largest Air Force Base in the world (Eglin Air Force Base), the largest Naval Air Station in the world (Naval Air Station Pensacola), the Headquarters for the Tactical Air Command (Hurlburt Field), and probably a dozen more military bases. Not only were so many bases within Sykes' district, but the military also owned hundreds of thousands of acres of some of the most desirable land in the state, including some of the most pristine beachfront property anywhere in the world.

So, if a military retiree were looking for a place to spend his or her retirement years, one could do a lot worse than Florida's Panhandle, courtesy of the good Congressman.

Typically, when someone retires from the military at such a young age, he or she begins a second career, often as a Civil Servant – that is, as a government employee. This "double-dipping" is quite common, and indeed provides enough time to "retire" twice. But in my father's case, he retired. That is not to say that he never worked again, but typically it was only in brief stints when the family needed extra cash for one thing or another. He would work for a period of time long enough to earn the money necessary for a new car, a new roof, or whatever was needed at the time.

He did, though, take advantage of the GI Bill and, to his credit, earned a Bachelor's Degree in – of all things – Art. Pottery became his passion and he built a walk-in kiln at our home. He exhibited his wares at many "Sidewalk Art Festivals" throughout the state, never making enough money to say he was "making a living," but he enjoyed it and was quite good at his craft.

At the time that my father retired, many of the psychological illnesses which are now taken for granted were not recognized and often were considered signs of "weakness." It is highly likely that my father suffered from Post-Traumatic-Stress-Disorder (PTSD), but this condition was not even identified until 1980. Certainly, upon reading the symptoms associated with PTSD, there is very little doubt that my father suffered from this malady, but never sought treatment.

My paternal grandmother died when my father was not even ten years old. My grandfather, by all accounts, had a nervous breakdown and abandoned my father, his only son. An orphan, my father was raised by relatives and probably spent time in orphanages. He never graduated from high school, but later earned his G.E.D. It is not unreasonable to believe that taking refuge by joining the Marines may have seemed like one of few good options available to him.

My father was named after his father, and was thus "George Ernest Devitt, Jr."

Given that his father abandoned him and left him an orphan, it remains a curiosity to me that he gave the same name to me, his only son: "George Ernest Devitt III." It did, however, give him a chuckle when someone would call our home asking "Is George in?" My father's response was "George Junior?" Of course, the caller assumed that it was the son who must be "George Junior." When the caller said "Yes, please," my father got quite a rise by simply saying "Speaking." An intimidating presence to my elementary school friends already, this attempt at humor did little to improve matters.

Interestingly, our family later learned that my paternal grandfather actually re-married and had another entire family. We learned that he passed away in the late 1960's, but regrettably, we didn't learn of this until after my father's passing in 2007.

My father and I did not have a close relationship. In fact, I can recall making telephone calls home during college and as a young working professional, and if my father answered, simply hanging up. I was about 40 years old before I had the courage to utter the words "I love you" to my father. The "build up" of my courage and my speaking the words which followed the "build-up," did not have the desired effect. The words were not spoken back to me in return.

I recall with vivid detail the events which led to my learning that my father wasn't the "color-blind," all-races-are-equal, man I thought he was. We had moved to Florida and my younger sisters had started dating. My father advised his daughters that if they ever went out with a black person, "not to bother coming home." I was crestfallen.   There weren't many things about my father that I respected, but my assumed understanding of his views on race was one of those few things. No doubt he made the comment while drinking, so perhaps it was the alcohol speaking and not him.   Because my father and I never engaged in any "deep" conversations, I never explored the subject with him.

I regret that I did not reconcile with my father prior to his passing away in 2007. It has been said that "...one can't give away that which he's never had..." If this is true, it explains a lot about the complicated relationship between my father and me and provides me with some understanding of why he rarely, if ever, demonstrated outward expressions of love. "You can't give away that which you've never had" – and as a child, he had never received much love.

Even in his last years, I had an unspoken admiration of my father's unique brand of "toughness." For many years, he was a two-pack-a-day smoker; with unfiltered Pall Mall's his "smoke" of choice. He and my mother – also a heavy smoker – eventually quit, but we were keenly aware of the risk both had of developing lung cancer.

In the late 1990's, because of some unusual coughing by my father, my mother insisted that he go to the doctor and get a chest X-ray. It was in 1998 that we learned that he had developed lung cancer.

My wife, Leslie, has spent her entire career as a healthcare professional in hospital settings. It was as gently as possible that she told me that lung cancer did not have a very high survival rate associated with it. "You don't know my father," I said back – only half-joking.

My father made it clear that if "survival" meant spending the rest of his life towing an oxygen tank with him everywhere he went – that he wasn't interested in surviving.

The doctors told him that the only chance for survival would be by the removal of a lobe from the cancer-ridden lung, with the hope that the disease had not spread to his other lung, the "good" lung. And it was with that hope that he underwent surgery to remove a lobe from one of his lungs. I don't remember exactly how long it was after the surgery - but it seemed like only weeks – that he was climbing up and down a ladder putting a new roof on the house!

Frankly, I never knew anyone "tougher." And by that I don't mean that he was some kind of bar-room brawler. But he survived many events which surely would have resulted in death for almost any other man, beginning with the self-inflicted abuse of his body from many decades of excessive alcohol consumption and from smoking almost two packs of unfiltered Pall Mall cigarettes, the attack on his Rifle Company's Camp while in the DMZ and the resulting hand-to-hand combat in which he killed almost two dozen enemy soldiers with nothing more than a 7" dagger as his weapon, and the accidents resulting from his many DUIs/DWIs that sometimes broke almost every bone in his body. And now the reader can add to that list my father beating lung cancer – which, on average, has a survival rate of less than 5%.

When my sisters and I were all younger, we tried to guess how long each of our parents was likely to live. I don't recall what we thought as a group, but I remember thinking – and believing – that every year beyond age 60 for each of them was a "bonus." A blessing, really. My mother lived to age 74, and my father until age 76. That amounts to thirty bonus years with which we were blessed!

To my astonishment, he was dutiful about going for the regular check-ups after his lung cancer surgery that the doctors recommended.

And so it came as a surprise to me when one of my sisters told me that she had learned on one of her many visits to my father, the he told her that he had visited his doctor out of concern that he was having to urinate frequently during the night hours when he was sleeping.

It was during this visit that the physicians determined that his lung cancer had returned and had, in fact, metastasized to his brain.

But by the time of this visit to his doctors, it was too late. The cancer now riddled his body. He put up a brave fight, but succumbed in August, 2007, about twenty months after my mother lost her own battle with cancer.

This failure to reconcile is a valuable, although regrettable, lesson that I learned. While a cliché, time is short.

Were I given the opportunity for a "do-over," I certainly would have managed the relationship with my father much differently and there would be far fewer unanswered questions about him, about our relationship, about his combat service, about his youth and what his feelings were about being abandoned by his father. The impact that such a dysfunctional upbringing had upon him had to have affected his entire life, and particularly his later years. And as his son, it certainly affected my own life.

Chapter 1

Transitioning from the North to the South

Moving from Massachusetts, where my very best friend was another black kid, what possible reason could I have for believing that blacks in the South were in any way *different* than those in the North? Soon after moving to Florida, and on the third and last bus ride to Hobbs Middle School, I felt something hit my feet. Reaching down, I saw that it was a yo-yo. I picked it up, put it in my pocket, and planned to take it to the school's Front Office and turn it in to the Lost & Found Department.

After getting off of the bus, another student – a black boy – approached me and said, "...you got my yo-yo?" My response, "...well, I may have your yo-yo. Can you describe..." was never completed. The sentence was never finished. I found myself on the ground covered in blood and by all accounts, with blood continuing to pour from my nose, my mouth and my ears. Someone finally broke up the fight – and characterizing it as a "fight" is giving my pugilistic skills far too much credit – and took us to the office. Upon arriving, the Principal, Mr. Helms, looking at my blood soaked clothes and face could only say, "George, did you even get in one lick?" Now having gone from a pretty low level of shame to an even lower level after Mr. Helms' comments, all I could say was, "No sir."

The boy who made his best effort to rearrange my face, Watry Barnes was suspended from school for five days. He was someone I didn't even know. Wishing I had been suspended as well, I went to school the next day with welts, bruises and dried blood all over my face. It was pretty clear who the victor was, and curiosity about every detail seemed to emanate from every single student...those I knew and those I didn't. I would gladly have remained at home - at least until the welts and bruises were not so obvious!

While I can't say that Watry and I ever became close friends, I can say that we did at least have a conversation in which – at least it seemed to me – he apologized. For the remaining five years that we went to school together, we at least said hello to each other when passing in the hallways or in the lunchroom.

To this day, I'm not sure if I handled the situation well or if I should have handled it differently. Clearly, I came off as the "Goody Two Shoes" in my lame efforts to identify the owner of the yo-yo. Perhaps I should've just handed the yo-yo to him. As I reflect on this event, I'm certain that I came across as – at a minimum – condescending. But there was a lesson learned. And it was my first lesson about how racial interactions were different in the South than they were in the North. I suppose that Watry, and most other black students at Hobbs Middle School, had enough of "being talked down to." And while that wasn't my intent, that's what I was doing. My guess is that had it been a white student who asked for the yo-yo, I would have asked the same question to make sure I was returning the yo-yo to its owner. But it's doubtful that a white student would have interpreted my question as "talking down to him." And my guess is that the situation would have ended with far less blood soaking my clothes. In fact, the white students whose curiosity I had to satisfy over and over all asked the same thing: "Why didn't you just give him the yo-yo?"

I know now that it's a good question.

My introduction to Santa Rosa County wasn't all bad. The beaches are breathtakingly beautiful. The sand is so white that, when we first moved there, in the fog of first awakening and looking out of my window, I thought it had snowed.

When we moved to Navarre Beach, I also had the opportunity to pursue my earliest efforts entrepreneurism. To be truthful and completely honest, I did not have any particular fondness for entrepreneurism, although I would later develop it as an adult. My fondness, frankly, was of money. And due to the combination of my age (I was too young to get a work permit) and the dearth of businesses on Navarre Beach, I was forced to become an entrepreneur if I was to satisfy my desire for money.

I had a leaky, but functional, twelve-foot aluminum jon-boat with oar locks and oars. It had been given to me by an Air Force pilot who lived at the beach while stationed at Eglin Air Force Base. Unfortunately, he was transferred. But while I lost a "friend" (who was more than twice my age – today people would probably look upon his "adoption" of me as something untoward) who had two catamarans and would take me sailing whenever he went out. But I did gain a jon-boat – which he sold to me for $5.

My father – handy in many ways – had a knack for building crab traps out of chicken wire that were quite effective in their design at attracting crabs and having them enter the trap through the "right" holes.

After he finished with each trap, I tied one end of a rope to the trap and the other end of the rope to an empty plastic Clorox bottle. In the middle of the trap was where the bait – cut up mullet, croaker or some other fish – was placed. Through a clever design, the "blue crabs" would enter the trap through one of several openings hoping to get access to the dead fish.   But once entering the trap, the crabs fell from one chamber into another.   Once in the second chamber, the crabs could not get out.

Every morning, I would take out the jon-boat and check my traps.   Each one almost always had one or more crabs.   I would shake the crabs from the chamber in which they were trapped to the boat's floor, or   deck.   After   re-loading   the   bait compartment with some fresh cut fish, and finishing this routine with all of the traps, dropping each back into the water, I rowed to shore and put all of the crabs into a large "holding pen," also made of chicken wire and which dangled from the sea wall behind our   house   and   into   the   water.   My "marketing" was limited to placing a 3" x 5" sign on the bulletin board at the local KOA campground:

Live Blue Crabs

$1.00/dozen

939-2226

During the summers, cars were lined up and down the street leading to our home. I don't remember how much money I made that first summer, but at the time it seemed a princely sum!

I ran my "crab business" until I was old enough to get a "real" job. My first of these was at the Jiffy Mart, which was a type of "7-11" store just on the other side of the bridge - on the mainland. I was paid a full 75¢/hour, and spent my time stocking shelves, sweeping, mopping and completing various other chores. I thought I'd won the jackpot! I actually got a real paycheck, which in a manner of sorts validated that I had a "real" job. To this day, I still have my very first IRS Tax Return. I completed it myself, and I was every bit of 12-years-old.

After living on the island for about two years, construction began on the first "legitimate" hotel in Navarre Beach – a Holiday Inn. I worked as part of the construction crew of the hotel (really what I did was pick up trash and the concrete pieces which littered the construction site), and became a member of the hotel's staff upon its opening. I began in the kitchen as a dishwasher, graduated to the dining room as a busboy, from there to becoming a waiter and finally became the host. The hotel's manager insisted that I get a badge which identified me as the Maître d', but even at age 16 or 17, I was able to determine that this was, at best, a stretch.

It was at the Holiday Inn that I had my first opportunity to work closely – to interact with and get to know on a personal level – with black people. The Chef, who was really the boss, was Joe. And his assistant, what we would call today a sous-chef, was a guy who, to me, defined "cool." His name was Dewey and after the restaurant closed, he held court in the bar every night. I learned a lot from both, and frankly don't recall being aware that there were many differences between us that resulted from the fact that our skin colors were different. Joe and Dewey may have had issues with some other white people, but never with me. I just enjoyed being around them – especially Dewey – in the hopes that maybe some of that "cool" would rub off on me!

As much as I enjoyed Joe and Dewey, I was far too ambitious to believe that my highest career aspirations would be to work in a kitchen. While I enjoyed being with them, I was smarter than them. I was more ambitious than them. Without much thought, I just believed that I was *better* than them. It was never an issue...just "a fact." At least in the eye of my warped mind.

Chapter 2

"Whuppins" Were Commonplace

Despite Watry Barnes' ability to "beat the crap out me," I still didn't believe that there were any innate or intrinsic differences between white students and black students. Certainly, I didn't recall learning in my Science classes that Darwin made any distinctions regarding race as humans evolved and developed. Thus, I had no reason to believe that my experiences from living in Massachusetts were not transferable to Florida.

Our school had an "accelerated" program for those students who demonstrated an aptitude for academics, who got good grades and who scored well on standardized tests. I was fortunate enough to be selected for this program, along with about a dozen other students. I was surprised – and again, curious – that there were no blacks who were part of our group.

It was around this time that I started to sharpen my observations of the black students with whom I went to school. The first thing I noticed was that I found it difficult to understand what they were saying. I had a hard enough time understanding the white students with their extremely strong southern accents. But on top of that, the black students almost seemed to slur their words, had poor diction and clearly had no command of "The Queen's English." What I didn't understand and couldn't determine was *why* their speech was different. I do recall that there were always one or two black students who "spoke like white folks." In every case, these were students who had transferred to Milton from another part of the country. This wasn't uncommon given the number of military installations surrounding our school. At each of these bases, it was commonplace for military service members and their families to be transferred in and out with regularity. These black students who "spoke like white folks" were almost always treated with more respect and dignity than their black peers who had lived their entire lives in Milton or the surrounding communities.

In the early 1970's, the schools in our county practiced corporal punishment with regularity. Each of the male teachers had a paddle. Some took great pride in the design and characteristics of their paddles: drilling holes in the wood to reduce the air resistance, forming handles which looked like the bottom of a baseball bat, designing a large "head" so that the area struck would be larger. When a student had the bad fortune of being overheard speaking in class, being late for class, not having completed the assigned homework, etc., these were all just causes for a "whippin," or more accurately, a "whuppin."

Always done at a place and during a time when the maximum number of other students would observe, the student being disciplined was told to place both hands on a wall, lean forward at an angle and to spread his legs. The teacher administering the punishment would often take a big and dramatic "wind-up," more in a grand gesture than with the expectation that it would result in a more severe paddling. I never saw anyone receive more than three strikes with the "paddle," and the objective was to elicit tears or, better yet, outright crying. Frequently, in gym class, these students would show us the welts or bruises resulting from the punishment.

Remarkably, corporal punishment is still allowed in each of Florida's 67 counties and their respective school districts. No parental consent is required in advance, although some school districts have made this a requirement, and there are no rules regarding what instrument can be used for administering the punishment, although it is frequently a wood or fiberglass implement made by the teacher, community members or students in a wood-working or "shop" class.

Notably, while black students almost always comprise less than 20% of the student population, my recollection is that they represented at least three of every four students who received this particular form of corporal punishment.

Even at the youthful age of a seventh grader, it begged the question: why were black kids subjected to "whuppins" far more frequently than white students? Were they just born "bad?" Were they inherently or intrinsically born with a tendency to misbehave? Surely, I thought, this could not be the case.

Chapter 3

Athletics: The Great Race Equalizer

In the early 1970's, when my family moved to Florida's Panhandle, the state – in fact, the entire South – had abandoned segregation. Officially. Or at least it would appear that way to any casual observer.

It didn't take long for me to realize that black kids sat with other black kids during the lunch period. Similarly, white kids sat with white kids. This was true throughout the school day, beginning with the bus ride. While blacks were not relegated "to the back of the bus" as they had been only 10-15 years earlier, it was rare that a black kid would sit next to a white kid on the school bus. And as we moved from one classroom to another, the same was true.

On the playground or during recess, though, things were different. If there was a "pickup" game of basketball or if kids were passing the football to each other, it was not uncommon for blacks and whites to mix.

Certainly, as I got older and the sports activities became more organized, it was even more common for blacks and whites to mix. This was true during practices and during the games, but ended with any post-game activities.

While it would be inaccurate to say that blacks were superior athletes to whites across the board, clearly the number of blacks who held school records – which were prominently on display in the gymnasium – was disproportionately larger than the percentage of the overall population made up by blacks.

At the time I attended high school, the conversion from yards to meters hadn't yet taken place, so all of the track records were recorded in yards – although this was not ever noted in the display cases which contained the school's many trophies, ribbons and plaques.

As a freshman, I recall one muscle-bound black senior classman who also served as the janitor for the gymnasium. I never quite understood why this student,

Herman Hudson, was always seen with a "dry-mop" cleaning the floors of the gym.

We didn't have any kind of "work-study" program. Perhaps this was punishment for some misdeed he'd committed. While he was on the track team, I never saw him working out with the team. In fact, I never saw him work out. And yet, his physique was extraordinary – with barely any body fat. The only "exercise" I ever observed was the ever-present pushing of the dry-mop up and down the length of the gym floor. And yet Hudson was the holder of the school record for the 100-yard dash: 9.8 seconds. Today, the length of the same race would be measured in meters, and Herman's time would be over ten seconds. Despite that, at Milton High School in the early 1970's, the guy was the fastest we'd ever seen.

Looking back at that period, it's hard to imagine what his time would have been with a good coach, some training and a regular work-out regimen. His speed, coupled with his obvious strength, probably would have resulted in his excelling on the football field as well. But he wasn't even on the team.

Organized team sports brought blacks and whites together, at least for a period of time every day. It's hard to convey in words the important role that sports play in small towns in the South. Friday nights saw the football stadium fill to capacity, often with residents of the town who had no connection to the high school. "Down South," Friday nights in the fall were reserved for high school football.

Football was so important, in fact, that the school's head coach, Hurley Manning, lived with his family in a house that was actually on the campus. Not on the edge of the campus or the fringe of the campus, but smack-dab in the middle of the campus! Students had to go around his house to get from one classroom to another!

Coach Manning was a short and squat middle-aged man with a closely-cropped crew cut. And he was the closest thing to deity on the campus. At pep rallies, filled with humility, Coach Manning's only promise was "...that we won't embarrass y'all on Friday night..." And the Panthers did win the State's Championship in back-to-back years (1978-79), further solidifying Coach Manning's legendary reputation. But even when it didn't field a championship team, Coach Manning never embarrassed his fans. The Panthers could always be counted on to do well – even in "off" seasons.

It's hard today to imagine high school sports without black students on the various teams. But for the generations which grew up only seeing all-white professional sports teams: baseball, basketball, or football, the concept must seem difficult to comprehend.

In Florida's Panhandle, blacks playing on sports teams had nothing to do with efforts to achieve racial equality. It had everything to do with the desire to win. And if winning meant putting black students in the school's uniform, so be it. I have little doubt that in the early days of integrating high school sports, there must have been a great deal of gnashing of teeth among some of the students, teachers, administrators and alumni.

By the time my family had made its way to Navarre Beach, desegregation was the law of the land. But it still had not fully taken root, sometimes for reasons of simple practicality. For example, while institutionally, desegregation had been accomplished, from a societal perspective very little had changed. Black students – at least for the six years that I rode the buses to school – all still boarded at the same one bus stop. And that's because all (or almost all) of the black families lived so close to each other in this one area that this was their designated bus stop.

If a white family lived in the same neighborhood that most of the black families occupied, it would be their family's bus stop as well. Of course, while I lived in Santa Rosa County, that never happened. But because of the large number of military families in the area, there were some black families which lived in the more affluent neighborhoods and would thus have white neighbors. It may be that they simply didn't take the county's buses to school. Or perhaps they took buses on which I didn't ride, so I never saw them boarding.

I don't know if it's reasonable to conclude, then, that the black families which all lived in close proximity to each other in East Milton had "self-segregated." I feel confident in saying that the concentration of blacks in this one small part of town was a remnant of history – and certainly not because the government or the broader society insisted that these families do so. But did our society, especially in places such as this in the deep South, keep these families living there by not providing housing assistance to them so that they could leave that area and improve their lot in life? Improve the quality of the dwellings they occupied? Provide them with the opportunity to move to more attractive neighborhoods?

The question then is, "Did the black families which occupied this one small area in East Milton live there because they chose to? Did they, in fact, 'self segregate?'"

Or did these families stay in this one small area in East Milton because for generations, that's where their ancestors lived. And was this because, for example, that if one were able to track this back far enough, this was where the slaveholder chose to provide the land which he was mandated to give as part of the slaves being given their freedom? And because our society, unaware of this history (which is only "assumed" by me) never did anything to correct this injustice committed many decades prior?

And since these families had never been integrated at a "societal" level, black kids generally only spoke with other black kids. And if the generations of black kids which preceded them received an education which was sub-par when compared to the education afforded white kids of the same eras, does that explain why I had difficulty understanding what most of the black students with whom I went to school were saying? And continuing with the same line of thought, did that then affect how well they performed on standardized tests and in the classroom?

Was one of the "unintended consequences" of our society's failure to provide an opportunity for these black families - which were all concentrated in one particular area of East Milton, Florida -

to be provided assistance so that they could relocate to a nicer home in a better school district, that these black kids would never improve their language skills and thus would never get good classroom grades or get good scores on standardized tests?

Was it the proper role of our society to provide this particular group with the assistance to improve their "quality of life?" And is the answer to that question dependent upon whether these families all lived in close proximity to each other because they chose to – they had "self-selected" to live in a neighborhood which was not, and likely would never be, integrated? In fact, they chose segregation.

Or would the answer be different regarding society's responsibility if we knew, as a matter of fact, that these families lived in close proximity to each other because generations earlier the slaveholder who freed the ancestors of these families chose this small parcel of land in East Milton to be the land given as a result of the slaves being granted their freedom?

And it's for reasons such as this that issues of race are, for me, so complicated.

I'm certain that an impartial observer would say that progress in racial equality had been slow, but was happening. At an institutional level, I believe that this was true in the early 1970's, when the Devitt family moved to Florida.

But it is my conclusion that segregation was still alive and well at a societal level. And the reasons for this are enormously complicated, especially for someone such as I, who is sorely lacking in my understanding of the many complicating issues which arise in almost any discussion of race and who choose to examine only one small circumstance of one small aspect of this very broad issue.

It does seem to me that we must, as a society, determine the answers to these many unanswered questions. And upon doing this, we must, again as a society, determine what our responsibilities are. We must acknowledge that our responsibilities to aid in some areas of desegregation may be a function of our determination of whether a community chooses to "self-segregate," or if that community's segregation is a result of its being wronged by our society many generations earlier.

But what should we do – as a society – in the event that historical records are insufficient to answer many of these questions?

And so it is clear to me that while segregation cannot be mandated, it still exists. But I, for one, can't discern whether this is because blacks choose to self-segregate or because our society has not done enough to foster voluntary desegregation by blacks in the south.

And yet, my original conclusions which form the pretense for this book, remained unchanged: 1) That the blacks which I came to know in the South were very different from those which I knew in Massachusetts. 2) The Southern Black is not as "book smart" as the Northern Black. 3) And, as a rule, whites are smarter than blacks in both the North and the South. 4) And finally, that as of the time that I graduated from high school, I had not met, and did not believe there existed, a single black person whom I considered to be smarter than I.

I find no pride in my conviction regarding the truth of these conclusions. But I *believed* them to be true. I also believed that this circumstance must change – and indeed, in some areas had changed. But for areas such as East Milton, Florida, if these circumstances do not change, it is our society which will be reduced – will become "smaller" – as a consequence.

For our society to achieve harmony and to maintain its leadership position among all nations and to advance – these circumstances must change. And we should commit – as The Great Society which we are – to ensuring that future generations will be unable to draw the same conclusions that I did.

As members of this "Great Society," so named by President Lyndon B. Johnson, who advanced the cause of improving race relations more than any president since

Lincoln, it is incumbent upon us to "right the wrongs of our ancestors."

We owe those in our society who have not benefited from our nation's many advances to correct this travesty of justice.

Chapter 4

Dillon, South Carolina
My Mother, My Grandmother,
<u>and A Wage of $7 a Day</u>

My mother grew up in the Deep South. She was born and raised in Dillon, South Carolina. A small town with a population today of less than 7,000, Dillon is known by some because it is the home of "South of the Border." Anyone traveling north or south on Interstate 95 cannot avoid the billboards which began promoting "South of the Border" from more than 100 miles away in each direction. The name's reference, which is obvious to most but which had to be explained to me, is to the fact that Dillon is just south of the border between North Carolina and South Carolina. "South of the Border" is a tourist trap comprised of souvenir shops, restaurants, snack bars, an over-priced gasoline station and public restrooms. And just to make sure that drivers made the connection with the other "South of the Border" – the one between the United States and its neighbor to the south, Mexico, the signs made it clear: "*Pedro says*: only 100 miles to South of the Border!" Dillon was, indeed, "south of the border."

In addition to "South of the Border," Dillon now proudly claims to be the hometown of the former Chairman of the Federal Reserve, Ben Bernanke. While not born in Dillon, Bernanke was brought up there and graduated as Valedictorian from Dillon High School. The Bernanke family, interestingly, was one of the few Jewish families in Dillon. In fact, Jewish families were so rare in Dillon that I don't recall ever knowing any. Bernanke was one of many teenagers who began their career working at "South of the Border." To defray the costs of his undergraduate education at Harvard, Bernanke worked summers at "South of the Border."

Dillon was also "tobacco country," and my mother's family and extended family made its living from this plant which, it would be learned later, caused over 150,000 deaths a year in the United States alone. The number who die from lung cancer, which results largely from smoking cigarettes containing tobacco, exceeds deaths resulting from any other form of cancer. And these statistics are thirty years after the highly visible "Surgeon General's Warning" required cigarette manufacturers to print – right on the package of the cigarettes – that smoking will likely result in an unpleasant death.

Of course, at the time that my mother's family began growing this crop, knowledge of the harm that would be caused by cigarettes was not known or not widely known. And the same land that grew tobacco would be used to grow cotton in other years. This "crop rotation" ensured that the soil remained fertile year after year, and has been practiced since ancient times.

My mother was proud to call Dillon home. She was one of four girls in her family, and her relationship with them and with her mother was, to say the least, complicated.

Long periods would pass without her speaking with her mother or with one or more of her sisters. This odd stubbornness afflicted her sisters as well. One, Joan, predeceased her and died by suicide. Her surviving sisters, Jean and Betty, have not spoken in years. I have often commented that "I want to grab each of them and shake them!" Each is about 80 years old and obviously will not enjoy much more time on this earth. I have no idea why they don't speak, but I have great confidence that the one who survives the other will carry guilt associated with this stubbornness to her grave. Curiously, when my mother passed away in 2005 after losing a long battle with pancreatic cancer, none of her surviving relatives – save one niece, Donna Jo – attended her funeral.

My mother was raised in a beautiful antebellum home in Dillon. Unfortunately, a fire caused the total destruction of their home. All that remains are grainy and blurry black and white photographs.

While not a woman of "privilege," my mother grew up comfortably due to her family's vast holdings in land well-suited for growing a variety of crops. Attending college, in general and particularly for women, was not as common during the period that my parents were of college-age as it is now. In 1950, less than one-in-ten adults completed a four-year college degree. By 1990, this had risen to one-in-four adults. Not surprisingly, men graduated at a higher rate than women and whites graduated at a higher rate than blacks.

But by this one measure of social status, my mother's family was above average. We were never close to relatives of either of our parents, but for what are obvious reasons, we were closer to my mother's relatives than those of my father. My mother did not complete college; nor did her mother. But I am aware that my grandmother had brothers who completed college at such excellent southern institutions as Wofford College and Presbyterian College. We all took a special pride in one of my mother's uncles who earned a Ph.D. and retired as a Professor Emeritus at Duke University.

Somehow, my mother ended up living as a single woman in Washington, D.C., where she met my father. They would marry and despite many rough patches, remained married for almost fifty years. Several things would come to light as my sisters and I grew older. For one, my mother was "with child" when she married my father. My parents never celebrated their anniversary, and I suspect that this is the reason. We also learned that each of my parents had been married once before marrying each other. In fact, my father had a daughter from his first marriage. We never met her, and neither prior marriage was ever discussed. But it is highly likely that I have a half-sister somewhere on this earth.

Growing up, my mother's family always had household help. And the help were always black people. During two brief periods that our own family lived in Dillon, we too had household help. It would be less than honest to say that our household help were "treated as family." But my mother did treat those who helped us with courtesy and with respect. I only recall one occasion which was unpleasant. A piece of jewelry – a ring or bracelet – was missing. It was assumed that our maid had stolen it. Even at the time, and I was only six or seven, I recall thinking that this assumption was unfair. My mother did end up firing the woman, despite the fact that there was no evidence or proof that she had stolen the missing jewelry.

My maternal grandmother, Marie Thompson Hamer, later lived in a small brick home constructed directly in the middle of her tobacco fields. As a young boy of 5 or 6 visiting my Grandmother during the summers, I could observe from her porch the field workers who were harvesting the tobacco under the scorching South Carolina sun. It was hard not to notice that all of the workers were black. As a six-year old, I envied these workers who were paid seven dollars a day for their labor. To me, that seemed like an enormous sum, and I asked every year if I could spend a summer with my grandmother – picking tobacco. Now, reflecting on that period, I realize that I probably would not survive even a single twelve-hour day in that scorching heat. And while to a six-year-old, $7.00 a day seemed like a princely sum, hindsight provides me with the benefit of knowing what an exploitative wage my "kin folk" were actually paying.

While I'm certain my grandmother had her own prejudices, I never heard her utter the word "nigger."

But in the early 1960's, terminologies were not well defined. Clearly, "nigger" was used as a degrading term. The terminology was confusing and words would sometimes be offensive when that was not the intent. For example, today the words "Negro" and "colored" may be considered offensive, but in the late 1950's and early 1960's, the words were often used without the intent of denigration. But my dear grandmother couldn't get it right, and her pronunciation of the worker in her fields came out as "nig-row." The "proper" terminology was clearly not sorted out during this period. "Colored people" seemed to be acceptable, as did "negro." But it was rare that the term "black" was used, and unheard of that the term African-American was used.

There was one occasion – the only instance that I recall affecting me – when one of the field workers asked to use my Grandmother's bathroom and she unhesitatingly said "no." I asked her why she wouldn't let the worker use her bathroom, and she told me that "it just isn't done." There was no malice in her voice at all. "It just isn't done."

But it did affect me. It disturbed me. Fortunately, I was at an age which resulted in my just barely missing seeing the signs designating separate bathrooms for blacks and for whites, or water fountains that said "Whites Only." So it was unpleasant – it was uncomfortable – to hear my own sweet grandmother refuse to share her bathroom with someone who not only asked politely, but who worked for her. But "it just wasn't done."

When I visited my grandmother and other relatives in Dillon, I played with other boys and visited with my cousins who lived nearby. Our groups were always comprised of only whites, but I don't ever recall being prohibited from playing with black children. And I have no memory of the ugly and overt racism that we could see on television. I'm sure that the word "nigger" was used, but I can't recall a single instance of its use by my relatives.

Chapter 5

Holley, Florida and a "Dream Home"

Later, in my teens, I do have memories of the term "nigger" being used. It was used quite intentionally for its "shock value." Many times, I was confident that the teenagers who used the term were not at all racist, but in a perverse way were attempting to create the perception that they were. Some even claimed to be members of the KKK. Without intending to minimize the wretched history of the Klan, or even of some factions which remain to this day, these teens were claiming to be members because they thought it was "cool," not because they ascribed to the Klan's tenets. In fact, they probably did not even know what the tenets were – except that members of the Klan didn't like black people.

Regrettably, similar scenes are repeated every day by people without a racist bone in their bodies when they tell a joke in which African-Americans, Asian-Americans or Hispanics are depicted stereotypically. While inexcusable, it is my belief that these jokes depict thoughtlessness more than they depict racism. And I use the term "thoughtlessness" to mean simply "without thought." If the person telling the joke actually "thought" about how hurtful or demeaning his or her words could be, they would likely not cross his or her lips. Unfortunately, too many of us are guilty of speaking "without thought." I count myself a member of this group – and my "membership" is not something of which I'm proud. I can say that I am far more conscious of how demeaning these slurs are and that I don't even recall the last time I told a joke or a story with racist overtones.

After living on Santa Rosa Island for several years, my father decided that he wanted to build his "dream home." When most people use the expression "...we're going to build our dream home," they mean that they want to have a custom home built *for* them. Being mechanically inclined and gifted at working with wood, my father's use of the expression was quite literal: he had every intention of building the home on his own.   After months spent poring over magazines which sell blueprints to be used for building a home, my father finally settled on "his" dream home – a beautiful Mediterranean style structure.

Of course, a prerequisite to building a home is owning the property on which to build it. The house on Navarre Beach which we'd called "home" since arriving in Florida was rented, so our family did not own any property. Because property on Santa Rosa Island was expensive when evaluated on a "per-acre" basis, my father decided that it would be foolhardy to purchase land in Navarre Beach.

Even putting the "price-per-acre" issue aside, the manner in which the civic leaders established land ownership on Santa Rosa Island was "unique." As a point of fact, no one could "own" property on Santa Rosa Island in Navarre Beach. Rather, "homeowners" entered into a 99-year lease of the property with the County. Had there been a shred of hope remaining that my father could stay on the island and have his dream home, this condition killed it.

Even today, some 45 years after the Devitt's were deciding what to build and where to build it, I'm not sure I can explain the rationale behind the 99-year lease notion that the County Fathers implemented. Nonetheless, people were "buying" property on the island as soon as it came on the market. And at the time, a Gulf-front lot would typically sell for about $20,000. Today, that same lot would sell for 25 times that amount – despite the fact that the "buyer" was actually a "lessor." Navarre Beach was known at the time as "Florida's Best Kept Secret" – and it was a well-kept secret. Only two families lived on the island year 'round and there were no condominiums or resort hotels until the late 1970's. Navarre Beach is definitely not a secret anymore! At the time we lived there, one hotel existed, and it was adjacent to the pier and provided a place for fisherman to stay overnight. The notion of a "resort" hotel seemed almost silly.

On one end of Navarre Beach was the pier and its adjacent hotel, and at the other end was a KOA campground. In between were a smattering of perhaps a dozen or more homes, almost all of which were vacant except during the summer months. Having decided that spending $20,000 for a puny lot that wasn't even owned, but leased, was folly, my father began his quest for property on which he could build his dream home. Of course, as luck would have it, there probably was no better property investment in the entire state at that time than Navarre Beach. Today, the hamlet which in the early 1970's was nothing but sand dunes and sea oats is now wall-to-wall condominiums and beach mansions. But about five miles north of Navarre Beach, squeezed in between a series of bays and rivers, was the community of Holley, Florida.

To provide perspective, the largest phone book in Santa Rosa County was that for the City of Milton. Within the Milton phone book were sections dedicated to Milton's surrounding communities. The entire phone book was less than ½" thick. In fact, to place a local phone call only required dialing the last four digits of the phone number being called. It was within this directory that Holley and Navarre had their combined assemblage of telephone numbers. Adding the households of both communities together, Holley and Navarre still filled only one full page and one-fourth of another page.

It was in Holley that my father found the property on which he would build his dream home. The property was actually four adjoining lots, which together amounted to slightly less than an acre.

Conveniently enough, we found a house for rent that was only about 500 feet from the newly-purchased property. Believing that the risk of losing equipment, tools or materials would be reduced by living close to the building site – and saving the "drive time" from Navarre to Holley and back every day – the Devitt's left our home on Santa Rosa Island and rented the house near our new property in Holley. The house had two or three bedrooms - depending upon how the rooms were counted - and one bathroom. Not particularly attractive, it was a house similar to many that can be observed while driving through the rural south. It was perched on cinder blocks positioned at each corner and had a barely perceptible "sag" in the middle – between the cinder block corners. There was no driveway and no grass. On the bright side, the red clay required very little maintenance or yard work. On the downside, it had no air conditioning. And while we knew that this would make the summers uncomfortable, the assumption was that the period that we would occupy the rental home would be a brief one. And the rent was only $65 a month, meaning that more money could be applied to the cost of construction of the new home. With a family of seven, it would be cozy. But surely we could endure cramped quarters for a period that would likely only be a few months.

The Holley Elementary School was, from all outward appearances, a charming school house. Without air conditioning, it could not have been a comfortable environment for learning. There were six rooms, one for each of the grades 1 through 6. One of my sisters recalls the shock she felt upon realizing that many of the students came to school in their bare feet. While our parents were certainly not wealthy, they did always ensure that we wore shoes, socks and clean clothes to school each day.

Holley is not an affluent community, and when we moved to the area, we became aware that some of our schoolmates lived in homes with only dirt as floors. But to the casual observer passing through, the town had and still retains a certain charm and rural ambience.

The property we bought had never been used, so the first order of business was to clear the land. With a small bulldozer, this task might take about half of a day. But doing everything by hand turned a half-day job into a summer's worth of back-breaking work. Florida is home to a plant known as the Palmetto bush. These smallish plants had leaves similar to those of a palm tree, and a large plant might rise to a height of three or four feet. The four lots which were to be cleared had several hundred Palmetto bushes. The plant has a "survivor's" root structure (this is the author's choice of terms – not those of a botanist). The term "survivor" is appropriate because these plants managed to remain in place through even the most wicked hurricanes which strike the area. And as we learned, the root goes straight down and then forms an upside-down "T." This made the plant virtually impervious to removal. One didn't just "pull out" a Palmetto bush. After learning that this preferred method wasn't feasible, we tried attaching one end of a rope to the bush and the other end of the rope to a manual winch. After seeing rope after rope snap, we replaced the rope with a chain. The chain didn't snap as had the repeated use of ropes of various diameters. Instead, the winch motor burned up. Replacing the winch with a bigger, stronger winch seemed appropriate. That is, until the motors of several successively larger winches also burned up, one after another. The next step involved attaching one end of the chain to the plant and the other end directly to our truck. This technique actually worked for the first dozen or so plants. Eventually, the transmission gears were "stripped" to the point that the transmission required replacement. Finally, we elected to dig out each plant by burrowing down to the level of the inverted "T" which was the root. The process was time-consuming, but eventually we did remove every Palmetto bush from the property. We were able to save whatever the cost of renting a bulldozer for a half-day would have been. Without renting equipment or hiring anyone to help the two of us, we wasted an entire summer on this exercise.

In Massachusetts, almost every home had a basement. In fact, the basement of our home in Springfield was where my bedroom was built. In Florida, basements are rare. Perhaps a better term would be "unheard of." Because the water table is so close to ground-level, anyone with plans to build a basement should plan on its flooding regularly. But my father believed that the slope of our property was such that a basement could be built with confidence that it would not flood.

With the use of a rented backhoe, digging a basement would be completed in a matter of hours. But, as with the clearing of the property, my father elected to dig the basement with nothing more than a shovel. We were certainly saving money on equipment rentals, but digging the basement with a shovel used up another summer. Once the basement digging was completed, the footings and foundation were poured and concrete blocks were used to finish most of the basement walls. It was somewhere around this time that my father became bored with building his "dream home."

It was maddening that, after spending so much time in the hot and humid Florida summers clearing the property and digging the hole for the basement, he just quit. "Quitting" was a pattern which would be repeated often by my father. It characterized jobs he had after his retirement, the period of time that he was a "dedicated" potter, the time he spent fishing in the Santa Rosa Sound and Pensacola Bay, and on and on. My recollections are admittedly harsh, and it would be easy to paint a picture of a decorated war hero who grew up an orphan and became a "Career Marine" who served our country in two wars. But most of that history – the more admirable history – happened either before I was born or while I was very young. As a teenager and young adult, I confess that my recollections about my father are not flattering.

My father's pension from the Marine Corps amounted to about $700 a month. Under almost any circumstances, an income of $700 a month for a family of seven would result in a "tight budget." But with no other income, and with bills abnormally high due to the cost of construction, the budget was extremely tight. It was so tight, in fact, that my mother returned to work after twenty years as a homemaker. Using her income as a secretary and using two of the four lots as collateral, she qualified for a home loan on her own. She then found a builder, picked out the house she wanted from an assortment of plans provided by the builder, and had a house built. While not as opulent as the "dream home," the brick ranch-style home was attractive and quite a step up from the $65/month rental home. My parents stayed in the home for over thirty years, and it was where each of them passed away.

As a reminder of my father's dream home, the back two lots were taken up by the hole in the earth that was to be a basement. Unfortunately, it was too far from the house to be converted into a pool, although considerable thought was given to that notion. For over three decades, this eyesore was always referred to as "George's Folly" by my mother.

Holley, at least in the mid-1970's, did not count a single black person among its residents. Almost every home, however, did have a pick-up truck parked in front of it. And the town did not lack for Confederate flags.

As it happens, Holley is surrounded by land owned by the Department of Defense. Some of the land was property of the U.S. Air Force and some of it was the property of the U.S. Navy. In fact, the Navy had a small outpost that was within a few miles of Holley. For anyone stationed at this small airfield and who did not live in Holley, it required at least an hour's drive each way to get there.

A black Chief Petty Officer was stationed at this post – known as Holley Field. Not wanting to endure the long drive from Pensacola, Milton or another surrounding city, the Chief and his family bought a modest, but nice, home in Holley. Certainly he could not have known that there were no other black residents in Holley. After moving in, the family received repeated threats that their home would be set on fire, that their children would be harmed or that some other harm would be inflicted. Eventually, someone did make good on one of the many threats and ignited a fire which destroyed the house. Fortunately, no one was home at the time. Obviously fearful for his family's safety and cognizant that it was only a matter of good fortune that no one had been harmed, he and his family left Holley and moved to Pensacola. He continued, however, to work at Holley Field and was hopeful that the County Sheriff would identify the individual or group responsible. No one was ever charged with the crime, but the message was clear that blacks were not welcome in the town of Holley, Florida.

As I recount this story, it seems as though it surely must have been an event from the 1950's or 1960's, but in fact occurred during the early 1970's. This unthinkable act happened *during my lifetime* and was almost certainly carried out by *someone known to me*. As I compose this, it is 2013. The town of Holley has grown significantly in population since the time of the arson. Much of the land is highly desirable waterfront property with beautiful bay views. And yet, with all of the growth enjoyed by the community, there is likely still not a single black family which resides within the Town Limits.

The U.S. Census has merged Holley with Navarre – Navarre is the community on the mainland just across the sound from Navarre Beach. It has grown at an even faster pace than Holley, and is marked by an eight-lane stretch of U.S. Highway 98 which passes through it. On either side are trailer parks, apartments and a fairly large number of homes.

Navarre is much more transient in nature than is Holley, and there are black families which call Navarre their home. But because the Census data does not separate Holley from Navarre, it is not a reliable gauge of the characteristics of either town, and examining this data and drawing conclusions about either town is, at best, ill-advised due to the fact that the census data is a blend of both towns.

Chapter 6

An Uncomfortable Confession

I don't recall the precise moment in time or the event which led to the shift in my thinking that black people, in general, are not as intelligent as white people. Indeed, I don't recall any black students ranking high among my high school graduating class. I don't have any memory of black students being in any of the advanced classes while in high school.

I can honestly say that, at least in my world, it was my belief *that whites were smarter than blacks.* Certainly, I thought that there were exceptions to this "rule," but they were few. I'm not proud that I held this view, but I know that my experiences in Florida's Panhandle as a youth are what caused me to gravitate to this belief.

And as a result, I confess that I felt "different" being in the company of black people. I felt uncomfortable. The life experiences of a black seventh-grader at Hobbs Middle School were very different than the life experiences of a white seventh-grader at Hobbs.

Even though my family could be considered economically disadvantaged, a characteristic likely shared with most black families in the area at that time, it still seemed as though my white family had little in common with the black families whose children all boarded the school bus at the same stop. According to 1975 Census data, the poverty threshold for a family of seven was approximately $9,000 a year – which is about how much my father's pension amounted to.

Surely, if my beliefs were correct – which is an assumption that alone is hard to swallow – then it must mean that a) blacks were innately inferior in any common measure of intelligence, or b) blacks were not provided with the same quality of education as whites, or c) that the environment in which black children lived was not as beneficial in some ways as the environment in which white children lived. Surely a case could be made in support of (b) and (c). In fact, those factors are what led to the Affirmative Action programs and other remedies which were intended to "level the playing field." One needn't have a Doctorate in Sociology to make that argument. But how long are these remedies necessary to correct the obvious injustices that black children endured? And as a practical matter, how does one know that assumption (a) isn't true, even if we accept assumptions (b) and (c) as "givens."

For example, I'm not certain that it would be difficult for me to admit that, "as a rule," Asian-Americans and Indian-Americans are more intelligent than white people.

The fact is that I am not a sociologist. All I know is that I believed I was smarter than the black kids I went to school with. I scored higher on standardized tests and I had a higher Grade Point Average. Going a step further, my conviction was that, "as a rule," white kids were smarter than black kids. And if my declarations were not true, it's only because I never came in contact with or associated with black people who had higher SAT scores or higher Grade Point Averages than I did. Can I admit that, almost certainly, there must be black kids of whom this was true? Absolutely. But "...as a rule..."

Looking back, I regret that I finished four years of high school in Milton, Florida, without having a single black friend. The very fact is abominable. And where does the blame for this abomination belong?

Chapter 7

Off to College

I can reflect upon my own children's journey to college. As parents, we were involved in their college selection process. We accompanied them to Orientation. We went with them and helped them move into their dorm rooms and "get settled."

This was not my experience. In fact, my own parents were so uninvolved that I'm not certain they even knew where I planned to attend college. Much of their lives, sadly, was viewed through the haze of alcoholism. They bore no financial responsibility and made no financial contribution to the cost of my undergraduate education. I didn't have the benefit of attending "Orientation." I took a Greyhound bus from Pensacola, Florida, to Gainesville so as to arrive a week before classes were scheduled to begin. When I stepped off the bus, it was my first time breathing the air of my new hometown.

My parents weren't sober enough to even give me a ride to the Pensacola

Greyhound Station. But it's amazing how resilient and resourceful and capable a teenager can be when circumstances require it. I stepped off of that bus in Gainesville with all of my earthly possessions in a "foot locker." When I asked the attendants at the station in Gainesville where I might catch a cab, they laughed and said "You must be from a big city! Got no cabs here." Ironically, Gainesville *was* "the big city" for me. It was the largest city I could recall ever living in. And so, given directions to the university, I set out on my trek to the campus – lugging a foot locker that had to weigh fifty pounds if it weighed an ounce.

I made my way to Hume Hall, which was my assigned dormitory. Even though I'd never been to Gainesville, I felt that I knew my way around the university because of the hours and hours I spent reviewing every shred of literature I could get my hands on from the University. Upon arriving at Hume, I was told that my roommate had already arrived. After checking in and being given the key to my room, I started walking to Room 228-East.

And then it struck me. Why hadn't it occurred to me before? And for the few minutes that it took me to walk to my room, my thoughts were frozen and I was fixated on only one thing: What if I had a <u>black</u> roommate? Would I try to make up some excuse to change rooms so that I could have a white roommate? And if he was not in the room when I moved in, how would I even know what the color of his skin was?

I inserted the key and slowly unlocked the deadbolt and opened the door. Clearly, someone had moved in. But who was it? And, more importantly – at least at that very moment – the most immediate and pressing question was: what was the color of his skin?

It didn't take me long to realize that my roommate was black. The "velvet art" with well-endowed nude black women which decorated our room was an obvious "giveaway." Not much sleuth-work was required. My worst fears had come true. I had a black roommate. Had my world come to an end?

Eventually, of course, I met my roommate. Waymond Norman was also an incoming freshman and was from Ocala, Florida. Ocala is about thirty miles south of Gainesville. Despite my many fears, Waymond and I got along just fine. We didn't do much together, frankly, but when we were in the dorm at the same time, it became clear that all of my fears were unfounded. To the reader, this may seem obvious: "Of course everything was fine!" But to me, that conclusion was not so obvious, at least in advance.

I learned a lot from Waymond, a lean young man of about my height, with an elongated face and – although I didn't see the attraction – a "hit" with quite a few very attractive black women. I joined a fraternity, Delta Chi. And Waymond pledged one of the "black fraternities," Kappa Alpha Psi. The differences could not have been more stark. Officially, all fraternities banned hazing. But the ban, as best I could tell, didn't go beyond the paper upon which it was written. At least while I was a student, hazing was practiced by almost all fraternities. For my own fraternity, the hazing activities were pretty benign: sleep deprivation, humiliating pledges during "Hell Week," and forcing pledges to do push-ups as punishment for minor acts of "disobedience."

Kappa Alpha Psi – and, for the most part, the other black fraternities – brought hazing to a whole new level. It was not uncommon for a group of "Kappa" brothers to pound on our dorm room door in the middle of the night, drag Waymond into the hall and beat him with sticks until his body was covered with welts, bruises and blood. And, upon initiation, the newly-initiated were proudly "branded." _Branded_. The way horses or other animals are branded.

These new members of the "brotherhood" voluntarily subjected themselves to having third-degree burns put on their upper arms. In Waymond's case, his fraternity branded him with what looked like a "Z." I thought the beatings in the middle of the night were bad enough – until I saw Waymond's "brand." Ironically, the brand was a source of great pride for Waymond. It demonstrated that he had made it through a "Hell Week," which tested the initiate in a variety of ways – all severe. And it announced to the world that he was a "Brother" in a fraternity that was well-respected – at least among black students and many alumni.

But officially, hazing is banned.

I enjoyed my freshman year with Waymond. It was an education. But I still thought I was smarter than he was. In fact, I *knew* I was smarter than he was. I would run into Waymond from time-to-time on campus and our meetings were always met with a warm embrace. Waymond graduated on time, but we lost track of each other.

Other than my elementary school friend in Springfield, Waymond was the only other *true* friend whose skin color was brown that I had.

At the University of Florida I did meet and became casual friends with a number of other black people. One who came close to challenging my conviction that I'd never met a black person that I believed to be smarter than I was a certain James Cunningham. When I was privileged to be inducted into Florida Blue Key, Florida's premier leadership honorary society, James was its president. He was a third-year law student and was pretty darn smart. But I didn't think he was smarter than I. At the time, being selected for Blue Key was a big deal. For example, the class of which I was a part initiated only three people. Now Blue Key routinely inducts classes of fifty people at a time – and the requirements are not nearly as rigorous. But it remains a prestigious organization. And while there remain very few black members, it was hard to argue that the organization discriminated against blacks when the president himself was black!

James is now a successful practicing attorney and Partner with a prestigious Miami-based law firm. His success comes as no surprise to anyone who knew the man.

My decision to attend the University of Florida was not a difficult one. I knew that my parents would not be in a position to pay for my college education, and the difference between in-state tuition and out-of-state tuition limited my choices. While many of my friends who went to Florida

State University would argue the point, it was quite clear that – at least in 1976, the year of my high school graduation – the University of Florida was clearly the best of the public universities in the state.

I had worked the summer after my high school graduation with the naïve belief that I could earn enough to pay my tuition and other bills for my entire freshman year. I actually had two jobs. During the day I worked at the Navarre Beach Holiday Inn and at night I worked as the janitor at the Youth Center located on Hurlburt Field – a U.S. Air Force base which is now home to our nation's Tactical Air Command.

Many of my friends asked me how I could stand to have a job as a "janitor." For one thing, it had its advantages. As long as I cleaned the Youth Center after it closed at 9:00PM and before it opened at 9:00AM, the manager was happy. It was technically a six-hour shift, but I was allowed to leave whenever I finished. And it rarely took me more than three or four hours to clean the facility. In fact, I began to feel guilty. I felt that in some way I was "stealing" from the Youth Center. So I began *looking* for more things to do. One week I waxed the floors in the whole facility using an industrial floor buffer – a beast to handle if one hasn't done so before, although I had. I did one section of the Center each night, and finished by the end of the week.

There are so many ironies in life. While I thought I was a *slacker* and was *stealing* from the Center by not taking six hours to clean it, the Center Manager thought I "walked on water!" After I waxed the floors, he made a point of asking me to visit him during the day to pick up my paycheck.   But his agenda was that he wanted to introduce me to his boss and his boss's boss.   "Gentlemen, in the fifteen years I've managed the Center, we've never had a custodian as good as George. We're lucky to have him and I hope he'll come back next summer," he said to his managers. Somewhat sheepishly, I thanked the three of them and told them how much I appreciated the opportunity to work there.

But this was not my first stint as a janitor. When I was in the eighth grade, my father was the part-time janitor at the Eglin Air Force Base Hospital – a huge facility. He needed an "assistant," and I was tapped. He did pay me fairly, but his patience often wore thin, and his temper short. So if I made a mistake or took longer to accomplish something than he thought I should, his yelling could be heard throughout the entire hospital floor.

The work itself wasn't so great, either. When a patient vomited, I was the one who got the call to clean it up. Or if the Emergency Room had been visited upon by patients after a bad vehicle accident, I had the privilege of mopping up the blood. Most of the other work was, to me, routine. Emptying the trash, sweeping, vacuuming and cleaning the bathrooms. I didn't know better. I didn't know that I should be ashamed or embarrassed that I was a "janitor." But after seeing how others reacted when I told them what I did, I rarely told people what my job had been.

Between the two jobs, I saved almost $4,000 during the summer of 1976. According to the University's "Student Budget Worksheet," that was $400 more than I would need.

And so it was a rude awakening when, near the end of the first academic quarter, the money which I'd saved was almost gone. But I'd worked since I was twelve, so the fact that I would have to get a job while attending classes was not much of a concern.

One of the jobs I took was selling women's shoes at the local Belk-Lindsey Department Store. The job was from 6:30-9:30PM during the week and all day on Saturdays. It was a great job and paid commissions in addition to the hourly wage.

But far more valuable to me, although I did not anticipate it when I applied for the job, it was what I referred to as a "Target-Rich-Environment." For any 19-year-old college student with raging hormones, what better job could there be than working in a Women's Shoe Department? On any given night, it was not uncommon for me to ask a dozen or more co-eds for dates – almost all of whom turned me down. My co-workers asked me how I could handle that kind of rejection. I explained that my goal wasn't to get <u>twelve</u>

dates, it was to get <u>one</u>. And I figured that my odds were pretty good. And I was right.

There was, however, a significant issue that I had overlooked. I would take a second job which started at 11:30PM. Getting off work at Belk-Lindsey at 9:30PM didn't make for much of a "date night."

It did, though, help me to become more outgoing and gregarious than I typically was. It also taught me how to handle rejection. All of this would become valuable to me much later during my career.

Little known to most students at Florida, on the top two floors of the J. Wayne Reitz Student Union were 36 hotel rooms. Since I had worked at the Holiday Inn at Navarre Beach, I approached Mrs. Hirni, the Manager of the "Reitz Union Hotel" and asked if there were any open positions. She told me that the only opening was for a full-time "Night Auditor." This was not a student "Work-Study" program, but a full-time position as a "Career Service Employee" of the University. Coincidentally, I had been the Night Auditor at the Holiday Inn, so Mrs. Hirni offered me the position on the spot. My hours were from 11:30PM until 7:30AM from Sunday through Thursday nights.

While my financial problems were solved, my academic problems were just beginning. I was never at risk of being expelled, but my first-quarter Grade Point Average (GPA) of 3.76 wouldn't be seen again. My goals after I started working full-time on "the graveyard shift" were a) to sleep whenever I had a chance, and b) to keep my GPA just high enough that I would graduate. While I don't recommend this schedule for anyone working while attending college, it wasn't all bad.

I met some terrific people. Dr. Reitz, the prior President of the University and the man in whose honor the Student Union was named, had his office just behind the office in which I worked and would frequently stop by the desk and chat. Dr. O'Connell, who preceded Dr. Reitz as University President and went on to be Chief Justice of the Florida Supreme Court, was also a frequent guest of the "Reitz Union Hotel," and when checking in always asked me the same question: "George, how long do you think you're going to be able to keep up this schedule?" And my answer was always the same: "Until I graduate, Dr. O'Connell." In a supportive voice, he would always say "God Bless Ya...hope you make it..." as he walked toward the elevators to the hotel after checking in.

It was my good fortune that I knew the other "Career Service Employees" who worked in the Union. It would come to serve me well.

For any college student, the education extends well beyond what's learned in the classroom. And so it was for me. It was my first opportunity to be surrounded by a diverse student body where I was exposed to Asians, Indians – and Jews.

I wasn't aware of any Jewish students at my middle school or high school. In fact, it is an indication of how ignorant I was that I thought Judaism was just another denomination of Christianity...Jews, Catholics, Lutherans, Presbyterians, Episcopalians – I thought they were all variations of the same theme.

I had no idea that Jews were a wholly different religion, much less that they represented a culture unique to their religion. In fact, during my first week on campus I visited the various fraternities on "Frat Row." Speaking with a Fraternity Brother at one of the houses I visited, I asked, "How many fraternities are there at Florida?" He answered, "Well, if you don't count the Jewish fraternities, there are 28." At the time I was a practicing Catholic, and the first thought I had was "I wonder which one is the Catholic fraternity."

Because I'd spent most of my life until that time in an insular and quite small community in Florida's Panhandle, I was to exhibit my ignorance again and again.

Chapter 8

Good Fortune

The Career Placement Center was in the J. Wayne Reitz Student Union, as was the Alumni Development Center and other administrative offices. My connection with the Career Placement Center Director would come in particularly handy. At that time, during "Recruiting Season," students would begin lining up outside of the doors of the Reitz Union during the middle of the night so that – when I opened the doors at 7:00AM – near the end of my shift, they would be at the front of the line to sign up on each recruiting company's interviewing schedule.

I scheduled an appointment with Mr. Kern, the Placement Center's Director. After warmly welcoming me, Mr. Kern asked, "George, what can I do for you?" I explained my predicament. When I got off of work at 7:30AM, the sign-up sheets were already full. "Let me think about it, George. Stop by tomorrow morning." I stopped by the next morning after my shift ended. Mr.

Kern first asked if I had any ancestors who were Native American or any other minority group. I thought this an odd question, but he explained that some slots were reserved for minorities as part of government-mandated Affirmative Action programs. "Nope. At least not that I know of," I responded. But he had a solution. "George, let's do this. You tell me the five companies that you most want to interview with, and I'll put your name on those five interview lists before they're even posted. But I can only do it for five companies. You think about it and let me know which five companies are at the top of your list."

Feeling a flood of good fortune and gratitude for this incredible blessing, I set about composing my list. The five companies which I told Mr. Kern were at the top of my list were AT&T, Southeast Bank, Burdine's Department Stores, Procter & Gamble and IBM. Fortuitously, the same day that I gave Mr. Kern my list, *Business Week*'s cover had a picture of a crisply-folded white button-down shirt. Embroidered on the pocket was the blue IBM logo. The headline was "#1's Awesome

Strategy for the '80's." Immediately, IBM jumped to the top of my list and I began researching the company using every source possible.

When I got in the interview room, sitting across from me was a Senior Marketing Representative, Mr. Jackson, who had driven down from Jacksonville to conduct two days of interviews.

"How did you get in here?" was how he began the interview. Thrown aback, I had no idea what he meant. "I'm sorry, sir, but what do you mean?"

Mr. Jackson showed me the sign-up sheet, on which it was clearly noted: MINIMUM CUMULATIVE GPA OF 3.5 REQUIRED. He had a copy of my transcript in front of him and could clearly see that my GPA was well below 3.5. And so began my first "sales call." I was selling *hard*. How would I explain how my name was not only on the list, but at the top of the list? All I could think of was to tell the truth – which in hindsight shouldn't have required much thought. Unfortunately, it took the better part of our hour together for me to fully convey the sequence of circumstances which had been set in motion five years earlier and which resulted in my sitting across from him interviewing for a position with the company which was, perhaps, the most desirable employer for any college graduate that year. Apparently, it worked. The next call I got was from an Assistant Branch Manager in Atlanta named Jack Thayer. Mr. Thayer invited me to fly to Atlanta for more interviews.

And this is when I first became intimidated by Doug and Sharon – even though I'd not even met them! With his cordovan wing tips propped up on his desk and leaning back in his chair with his hands clasped behind his head, Mr. Thayer asked abruptly, "So why should I hire you, Devitt? I've already hired an Engineer from Georgia Tech and a graduate from Harvard. Why should I hire you?" I began selling. And selling even harder than I had with Mr. Jackson back in Gainesville. Before I finished my "sales pitch," Mr. Thayer got up and left the office without saying a word. In a few moments, he returned and said, "You're in luck. The

Branch Manager has a few minutes to meet with you." Mr. Thayer walked me down the hall to Mr. Boucher's office. Dave Boucher had been a Marketing Manager (one level below a Branch Manager) in Jacksonville and while there had been responsible for the University of Florida as an IBM customer. As I dove into my "sales pitch" explaining my poor grades, Mr. Boucher interrupted me and said, "Don't worry about your grades. I was a terrible student. Did you ever eat pizza at Leonardo's in Gainesville?" And so our brief time together was spent discussing Leonardo's unique recipe which included an abundance of cheese on its pizzas.

At the end of the day, Mr. Thayer said that he would be interviewing one more candidate on Friday, and that I would receive a call the following Monday with their decision – regardless of what it was.

My interview was on a Wednesday and I was to return to Gainesville on Thursday. This presented something of a problem for me. One of my practices was to send a type-written "Thank-You Letter" to the individuals with whom I had interviewed. Even if I had determined that I was no longer interested in the position, I never failed to complete this practice.

And so it was that I found myself alone in my hotel room, reflecting upon what had been a successful day from my viewpoint, and realizing that, due to my schedule, it would be impossible for me to ensure that a letter would arrive in the hands of Dave Boucher and Jack Thayer before they would make their decision. Somewhat despondent, I channeled my intense disappointment into an almost maniacal focus on how I could overcome this problem.

And then it occurred to me. I could send a Western Union telegram to each of them on Thursday, and it would be delivered the same day. And so, flush with the satisfaction that I'd come up with a solution to my problem, I picked up the phone to call Western Union. Not having ever used its services before, I was astonished at how expensive it was to send a telegram. I also now understood why, on television shows or in movies which depicted the use of telegrams, brevity was employed. Western Union charged by the word. When I'd completed composing the telegrams to Boucher and Thayer, the cost was over $200 for both (a pretty hefty sum for a college student in 1981)! Unhesitatingly, I placed the order, which would be delivered on Thursday morning.

It was also on Thursday morning that I began my return trip to Gainesville.

Arriving back in Gainesville earlier than expected, no sooner had I walked into my apartment than the telephone rang. It was Mr. Thayer. "Hey Devitt, got your wire. Congratulations, Devitt. You're going to be part of this year's 'litter.' Welcome to IBM!"

I was at once both overcome with happiness and had questions bouncing around within my mind: What was "a wire?" What about the candidate that they were to interview on Friday? When would I start? How much would I be paid?

But it was all I could do to utter some inane comment along the lines of "Thank you for your confidence in me, Mr. Thayer. You will not be disappointed."

Then he said, "Hang on a second. Someone wants to speak with you." It was then that I heard Mr. Boucher's voice: "Hey, just wanted to let you know I got your wire. Congratulations and welcome to the team!"

"Thank you sir. I look forward to joining your branch and to making a significant contribution."

"I'm sure you will, Devitt. Looking forward to seeing you in July!"

Then Mr. Thayer returned to the phone and said, "I'm going to FED-EX your Employment Package. You should receive it tomorrow. After you do, call me with any questions. Do you have any questions for me right now?"

"No sir. I look forward to speaking with you tomorrow."

Years later, I would learn that my sending the Western Union telegrams – or, as I would learn, "wires" – was the game-changer. Boucher, upon receiving his, walked into Thayer's office and told him to cancel Friday's interview and to get an offer letter out to me ASAP. But it was literally several years later that someone I met asked me "if I was the guy who sent the wire?" As it turns out, Boucher, a gregarious and enthusiastic manager who would go on to have a very successful career at IBM, upon receiving "the wire," was walking around the office and showing it to anyone who would listen. And thus, I became somewhat of a legend as being the "guy who sent the wire."

And, to this day, I have no doubt that it was this act that resulted in my being offered a job with IBM. It just goes to show that one can never predict what will "press the buttons of a decision-maker." It may be something, in fact, as innocuous as sending a telegram – done out of necessity rather than out of some well-thought-out plan – that has the desired impact.

On Friday, as promised, I did receive my Offer Letter. I would begin with IBM in its Atlanta Office on July 1st, 1981 – the same day as Doug (the Georgia Tech Engineer) and Sharon (the Harvard grad). My starting salary was to be $19,680 per year. While the salary was certainly acceptable, it was considerably lower than that offered by AT&T. But joining IBM had been my "dream job." And, as luck would have it, it was only shortly after receiving AT&T's offer that a certain Federal Judge whose name was Harold H. Greene would issue the ruling which would "break up" AT&T. The Bell Companies – the phone companies – would become independent of AT&T, which would provide long distance services, retain its manufacturing capabilities and the renowned Bell Labs operation. Over the next several years, over 100,000 people were laid off from AT&T. Had I accepted their job offer, which paid about 20% more than IBM, I most certainly would have been one of the casualties of the layoffs.

My decision to join IBM had nothing to do with this, and yet my life would have been vastly different had that been the path I chose.

I was clearly the beneficiary of unwarranted, but greatly appreciated, good fortune.

Chapter 9

Proud to be a Marine: First Into the Hotspots

It is typical for Marines who will be transferred to a combat post that they will be sent to the assigned theater's "hot-spots." While members of the military's other service branches may, for example, have been assigned to Da Nang or Saigon upon their arrival "in theater," my father was assigned to a Rifle Company which was encamped in the DMZ (the De-Militarized Zone). I've never understood why most people don't "get it" in recognizing this most obvious of contradictions – that some of the fiercest combat engagements took place in an area known as "The De-Militarized Zone."

Not widely known is the fact that the life expectancy of a Marine Corps Second Lieutenant who parachuted into the DMZ in the summer of 1967 – at the height of the conflict's hostilities – was three days. Three days. 72 hours.

When my father arrived "in theater," he learned that his Company had been trapped for weeks atop a hill in the heart of the DMZ. The Company had endured almost constant fire from the forces of the Viet Cong, and the combat-weary Marines were growing weak and fatigued, making them more vulnerable to enemy forces. Rations in the form of food and water, and such essential supplies as ammunition, were becoming increasingly scarce. The Company had set up a perimeter of razor wire and developed a schedule for sentry duty on posts around the camp's perimeter and with a detailed schedule of who rotated on and off shifts, guarding the make-shift camp which was in the middle of the hill and at its highest point.

One of the Marines who had sentry duty was so heavily fatigued that he fell asleep while on duty at his post. It was through this breach that the Viet Cong entered the camp with a dozen or more "suicide bombers."

On this moon-less night, the camp was pitch black in darkness. My father was asleep on the cot in his tent when the first of the Suicide Bombers entered -- dynamite strapped to his body. Upon entering my father's tent, the bomber detonated the explosives which were strapped to his body. Awakened by the sudden and unexpected explosion and blinded and rendered deaf by the force of the blast, my father was not immediately aware of what had just happened. Instinctively, he rolled under his cot and took cover. As he did, he felt around with his hands in an effort to locate his M-14 rifle and his own cache of hand-grenades. Remaining under his cot until some of his sight and hearing returned, he felt around in the night's darkness in an effort to locate his own weapons -- or anyone's weapons. He was only able to locate his dagger – which had a 7" blade. The might of this ordinarily heavily-armed United States Marine had been reduced to a 7" dagger which had probably not been sharpened in weeks.

Engaging the Viet Cong, which had by now overwhelmed the Marine Rifle Company, most Marines were forced into hand-to-hand combat with their enemy. In official Marine Corps documents made available years later, and upon their de-classification, it was noted "...that one Marine Gunnery Sergeant was able to kill almost twenty Viet Cong and North Vietnamese Regulars in hand-to-hand combat with only a single dagger as his weapon..." This reference was almost certainly to my father, as he was the only Gunnery Sergeant in the Company. It was this documentation, which was written by his Commanding Officer in a recommendation that my father be awarded the Silver Star, which is my family's only record of what happened on that fateful night. Certainly my father would never speak of those events.

The makeup of a fully-staffed Marine Corps Rifle Company would include between 150 and 200 Marines, the Company Commander (typically a Captain, or O-3), the Company Executive Officer (the XO), the First Sergeant and the Company Gunnery Sergeant – a billet filled by my father, in addition to three or four platoons, each led by a 2nd Lieutenant.

While astonishing beyond belief, contemporaneous reports were that only 5 – 10 Marines, from a company made up of 150 or more, would survive this attack. It is for this reason that, at the time, media reports were that the Company had been wiped out. In essence, it was wiped out, with only 5-10 surviving Marines from the original company still alive, all of whom suffered serious injuries. In fact, this was the understanding which my mother had *after* reading the news reports - but *before* receiving the postcard from my father which was sent from the hospital ship.

Unlike career veterans from the Army, Navy or the Air Force, retirees from the Marine Corps did not have the skills developed by members of the military's other branches which are often marketable and which may lead to a lucrative "second career." Infantry. Sniper. Gunnery specialist. None make for a compelling civilian resume.

Each branch of the Armed Services has an "elite" unit among its ranks. The Army has its Special Forces Groups and the Rangers. The Navy's elite are known now as the Naval Special Forces Group or SEALs. The Air Force has its Special Operations Command.

The total number of active duty military personnel is about 1.4 million. Of these, about 500,000 are members of the U.S. Army. The U.S. Air Force and the U.S. Navy are each comprised of about 300,000. About 200,000 Marines are on active duty at any given point in time. It is because of these force level counts that the Marines consider themselves to be "elite" in their entirety.

As one might expect, there is a healthy level of good-natured "ribbing" among and between the services. The fact that the Commandant of the Marine Corps reports to the Secretary of the Navy is the source of much teasing and ribbing.

Upon retiring, however, circumstances surrounding the retirement of a Non-Commissioned Officer whose decades of service are in the U.S. Marine Corps do not provide a particularly promising outlook for a "second career."

With the unique (and unusual) exception of the Marines' Judge Advocate General Corps, there is not the degree of specialization in the Marine Corps which exists in the other services.

The Marines are unique in that the entire Corps is combat-eligible (including the JAG Corps – the only military lawyers which are "line officers" and not "staff officers"). This one Marine, my father, was unique as well for the skill set which he developed during two decades of active duty. Marines are exceptional in one area unique to its service branch: killing. From its combat infantry to its cadre of superb "marksmen" and "sharp-shooters," the Marine is an extraordinary "killing machine." The 13-week Boot Camp to prepare each "recruit" to become a "Marine" is almost exclusively dedicated to honing the skills of the recruit to those of a trained killer. By way of example, virtually every Marine wears the medals for Rifle Marksman and Pistol Marksman.

Unless a family's father or another family member has been assigned to combat operations in a Marine Rifle Company or a smaller unit during the height of the hostilities which are characteristic of such major engagements as the Korean "conflict" (technically, a United Nations "police action," although 88% of the combatants were members of the U.S. Military forces) or what we refer to as the Vietnam War, any attempt to convey the feelings and emotions of the family members whose household head is now "incommunicato" some 10,000 miles from home is hopeless. As with the United States' involvement in Korea, the Vietnam War was also not a "war." Constitutionally, the power to declare war is reserved solely to the Congress of the United States, and there was no such Declaration of War against Vietnam ever passed by the U.S. Congress.

Clearly, the nature of combat operations which is observed by the current generation is vastly different from those in which the prior generation – my father's generation – was engaged. And of course, the generation which preceded my father's participated in an even more different type of operation.

Why do I consider this significant and worthy of taking note? It is simply this: the scale of the sacrifice of human lives is vastly different from generation to generation. It has been almost twelve years since the attacks of September 11, 2001. In the twelve intervening years, in essentially two separate wars, less than 7,500 of our dedicated forces have been lost.

By contrast, the entire duration of World War II was 45 months – less than four years. The Korean "War" had duration of 37 months, essentially three years. And yet, our nation lost the lives of over 400,000 military personnel in World War II, and some 36,500 in Korea. So – we observe and are engaged in much lengthier military campaigns now – with the number of casualties orders of magnitude lower.

Secondly, the nature of combat now is much different. Our forces now "fight from afar," whereas in World War II, Korea and Vietnam, combat was "up close and personal." By way of example, contrast the opening scene of Steven Spielberg's epic, "Saving Private Ryan," with the knowledge that many of the unarmed aircraft which fly above Afghanistan, Iraq (and controversially, many other sovereign countries) and which are known commonly as "drones," are controlled by operators in

United States military installations in, of all places, Nevada.

Thirdly, the skills required of those prosecuting combat operations today are significantly different from those in World War II, Korea and Vietnam. Today, the value of "technical skills" associated with the typical combatant is clearly a major change from the skills employed by warriors engaged in close-quarters, hand-to-hand combat.

What are the "takeaways" from my observations?

1) The racial profile of today's combatant is likely to be different. Because of the requirement for advanced technical skills today, it is likely that the nature and number of minorities which make up our combat forces will be significantly different.

2) The "enemy" which we confront today is much more amorphous than in World War II, Korea or Vietnam. In fact, today's military is engaged in "The Global War on

Terror." It has always been assumed that a military conflict requires at least two "identifiable" combatants which are "fighting each other." It begs the question: were we to "declare war," against whom would this declaration be made?

3) Prior wars "ended." There was an event which signified this "end," typically a "surrender" which described, in great details, the terms of this surrender. Will the "Global War on Terror" have an end-point? If so, what might this look like? Who would be "surrendering?" What – or who – would give the surrendering party, or parties, its authority?

There are many more questions than answers. But doesn't it seem that before the United States enters into negotiations surrounding any such "surrender," these questions should be addressed – and addressed *in advance*?

Is it likely that we will ever return to the type of combat operations which typified those of the generations which preceded our own? Is what we observe today "the new normal?"

Moreover, and <u>well</u> beyond the bounds of this book, how and when will we determine when it is appropriate to impose our nation's will upon other sovereign nations? What is the role of the United States? Are we the world's "Police Force?" For example, Saddam Hussein was a bad guy. But there are lots of "bad guys" who engage in acts of atrocity seemingly at will. Is it our role to stop all of these "bad guys?" And who, exactly, assigned this role to us? And as we develop our list of "bad guys" which we will rank-order from the worst to, somewhere on the list, the "best of the worst," what are the factors that will go into such a determination? And who, exactly, provides oversight related to <u>our</u> actions? And by the way, do we have the resources necessary to even *come close* to accomplishing this?

So...more questions than answers.

Without any deliberate attempt to diminish the sacrifices made by the members of the "other" United States Armed

Forces serving in Iraq and Afghanistan, but to provide some historical perspective, the United States and other "Coalition" forces were engaged in two (actually, many more than two) discreet combat operations for which, at best, the motives may be characterized as "confusing." Essentially, these were "Operation Iraqi Freedom" and "Operation Iraqi Liberation."

Separately, and with motives which may perhaps be characterized as "more just" and "less confusing," United States and "Coalition" combatants engaged in a military operation known commonly as "Operation Enduring Freedom" in Afghanistan. Similar to the military engagements in Iraq, U.S. and Coalition forces fought in far more combat operations than those which are most well-known, Operation Enduring Freedom (Afghanistan), Operation Iraqi Freedom, Operation Iraqi Liberation (Iraq).

Further, to provide additional perspective relative to the Korean Conflict, the Vietnam War, Operation Iraqi Freedom and Operation Iraqi Liberation, as well as the primary combat operation in

Afghanistan, Operation Enduring Freedom, the operations in Iraq and Afghanistan resulted in a loss of American lives which was orders of magnitude less than American fatalities resulting from combat operations in Korea and Vietnam.

The nature of today's combat operations is very different from that of prior generations. Technology plays a far greater role now that it did decades ago. And as long as African-American students, in particular, shun the technical disciplines of science and engineering, we are apt to have a fighting force which is "whiter" than ever.

Chapter 10

IBM: A New Brother and a New Sister;

Sharon Takes a Husband

Some of the things which caused me to be uncomfortable when in the company of black people are rather absurd. And the discomfort was invariably self-induced; I never can recall a black person intentionally making me feel uncomfortable.

By way of example, the woman to whom this book is dedicated, Sharon Malone, is an African-American of considerable distinction. She received her undergraduate degree from Harvard, worked for IBM upon graduation – which is where we met – and left IBM to attend Columbia Medical School. She completed her Residency in OB/GYN at George Washington University and, although only working part-time now, is one of the most respected gynecologists in the District of Columbia.

She also happens to be the sister of Vivian Malone. Vivian was one of the two black students that Governor George Wallace blocked from entering the University of Alabama. The courage it took to withstand such vitriol is beyond what I can comprehend.

Characteristic of Sharon's modesty – or perhaps because she gave Doug and me too much credit by assuming we knew who her sister was – I don't recall Sharon ever telling us about her older sister's achievements and fame. In fact, it wasn't until Doug and I attended a party hosted by Vivian and her husband Mack, at which I saw a framed Time Magazine cover featuring Vivian's picture, that I became aware of Vivian's prominent role in our nation's civil rights history.

I recently watched a documentary, *Crisis*, which was filmed contemporaneously about this watershed Civil Rights event. I'd never seen a picture of Vivian when she was young. But, as with the other Malone sisters whom I knew, she was breathtakingly beautiful. Moreover, as I watched this documentary, it's hard to imagine a twenty-year old enduring the intense glare from spotlights around the world. Poise. Confidence. Fearlessness.

At the time of this writing, I have three wonderful daughters, two of whom are grown. Kimberly, 22, has graduated from the University of Florida, and Ashley, 21, is beginning her senior year at Rice University in Houston. I cannot imagine their enduring the bright lights and the attention of the entire world, literally. And the very real potential of suffering physical harm. And having the conviction to undergo such travails not for the attention, but despite the attention brought upon them.

I joined IBM on the same day as Vivian's younger sister, Sharon, and with a Georgia Tech graduate named Doug Locker: July 1st, 1981. I confess that it took a lot to intimidate me, but being hired as one of this group did so.

We spent a full year in IBM's training program and became very close. In fact, we were as close to being brothers and sisters as is possible without sharing the same DNA. While I would not verbalize these feelings in Doug's presence, the three of us loved each other a great deal and there was nothing one of us would not do for another. Not only did we spend extended periods of time away together in training classes, we also had lunch together virtually every day and went out after work as a group with the same frequency.

Within a year or two of joining IBM, both Doug and Sharon had purchased condominiums – both on Peachtree Street in Atlanta's tony Midtown area. To this day, I don't know how Doug and Sharon managed to amass enough cash for the down-payment required to purchase a condominium. So while they were already "homeowners," I was still an "apartment dweller."

I don't recall being a profligate "spendthrift." In fact, I still drove the same car which I owned while in college, a 1974 Opel Manta. My Opel was the source of some good-natured "ribbing" by my colleagues.

For example, it did not have air conditioning. And if I were driving near the office where it was likely that I'd be seen by others from the IBM branch office, I was so embarrassed that I would drive with the windows rolled up. So, with sweat pouring down my face in the 95-degree heat, no one knew that I was without air conditioning.

I knew that eventually I would have to buy a better car. Taking clients to lunch in the Opel would at best be considered "poor form," and at worst, inconsiderate.

The Opel was lacking a number of other things as well, the most inconvenient of which was a starter. This non-functioning component was considered by me to be only a minor inconvenience. The Opel had a 5-speed manual transmission, so I was certain to always park on a hill so that I could "jump-start" the vehicle. With Atlanta's hilly terrain, finding a good, hilly spot for me to park the Opel was rarely difficult.

This went on without incident for more than a year after I'd moved to Atlanta. That is until one day when my boss, a no-nonsense former accountant whose name is Gale Crosley, asked me for a ride after work to pick up her car, which had been in the shop all day having some minor repairs completed. As Gale and I made our way to the parking garage, I warned her of the non-functioning air conditioner, but did not tell her that the car was also without a starter.

Making every effort to appear nonchalant, after letting Gale into the car, I began to push it out of its parking space and to face it in a downhill direction. "What in the world are you doing, Devitt?"

"Just need to give it a jump-start. No big deal." Then, standing next to the driver's side seat, with the door open, I gave it a mighty push and ran alongside of the car for about ten seconds before jumping in, "popping the clutch" and revving the engine. Off we were. Covered in perspiration dripping from what seemed like every pore in my body, Gale said, "Devitt, don't you think it's about time that you got a new car?

"Yes ma'am," was my immediate response. While neither of us said anything, the lack of air conditioning was now making an already tense situation even worse.

After about a ten-minute drive, we arrived at her mechanic's shop. Expecting a "thanks for the lift," or simply "thank you," what I heard instead was, "Devitt, that is the last time I will endure this. You make a decent living. Get a damn car!"

Courtesy of the IBM Credit Union, within a week I was driving a dark gray 1981 Honda Accord "Anniversary Edition." The designation, "Anniversary Edition," meant that this automobile – which had at one time been the very symbol of utopianism since it was first introduced in the United States market – had leather seats, power windows, power door locks and eight speakers. It even had an antenna that went up and down automatically! Most importantly, perhaps, it had a working starter and air conditioning which converted the car into a freezer.

Because the lunches which Sharon, Doug and I enjoyed almost always took longer than was allowed, we came up with the "oh-so-clever" idea of leaving our suit jackets draped on the chair-backs of the chairs at our desks. We might also leave our study materials out and open on our desk, further giving the illusion that we were "in the office," but had just stepped away from our desks. While we never knew if our "ruse" fooled anyone or not, we were never caught.

It was during these lunches that Sharon would further my "education." For example, it was during one of these lunches that I learned never, ever to pay for lunch or dinner while on a date with cash – always pay with a credit card. For Sharon, at least, such a *faux pas* would result in this being her suiter's first *and* last date. A man so gauche as to commit such an atrocity was not worthy of another opportunity. Sharon was a seemingly endless font of such lessons, all of which I soaked up.

We all lived and worked in Atlanta, and it was there that Sharon invited us to attend a party that her sister Vivian and Vivian's husband Mack were hosting. I'm not certain, but I'm pretty close to certain that Doug and I were the only white guests at this gathering of some of Atlanta's most successful and prominent black people. I can't speak for Doug, but I know that I felt a level of discomfort. It was the first time I'd experienced what it was like to be a "minority," and given the accomplishments and notoriety of those in attendance, referring to this as my experience as a "minority" is a bit of a stretch. Everyone there made Doug and me feel welcome, and yet I still felt that I was out of my element. And I was uncomfortable. But my discomfort was self-induced and resulted from my own insecurities. I will know that – at least for me – I will be truly "color blind" when the time comes that I am equally comfortable with black people as I am with white people.

The Malone's are an exceptional family. Not only was Vivian a key figure in the Civil Rights Movement, but Sharon has another sister, Margie, who was a successful IBM executive and who became the wife of a doctor who also happened to be a Medical School president. Sharon has a cousin, Jeff Malone, who was a star in the NBA.

The family's history is rooted in modest circumstances. Growing up in Mobile, Alabama, the age difference between the oldest child and the youngest child was significant. The oldest of the Malone siblings is Sharon's oldest brother, who as of this writing is 77 years old, fully 23 years older than Sharon. Sharon recalls her father taking her to school when he was almost 70 and it was often assumed by many that he was her grandfather, not her father. The Malone's father was a maintenance worker at a local military base and their mother was a maid. But Mr. and Mrs. Malone instilled in their children the importance of education – because they wanted a life for their children which was better than their own.

Sharon – and for that matter all of her sisters – is extraordinarily beautiful. Her beauty, coupled with her intellect, caused Doug and me to know that if and when she married, it would be someone who had to be able to "hold his own" with her.

I first met Sharon's husband-to-be while on a business trip to Washington, D.C., in 1992. Tall, handsome and with a commanding presence, he was at that time a sitting Judge. His commitment to public service had subsequently led him to become the United States Attorney for the District of Columbia, one of the two most powerful posts for a U.S. Attorney. Never one to shy away from a fight, he prosecuted Congressman Dan Rostenkowski, who at the time chaired the powerful House Ways and Means Committee, for corruption. When Sharon's beau was finished with Rostenkowski, the distinguished Congressman was behind bars. Continuing his public service, her beau served as Deputy Attorney General under Janet Reno in the Clinton Administration. He was so respected that George W. Bush asked him to stay on as Acting Attorney General until Bush selected a nominee who was confirmed by the Senate.

And while the family didn't worry about where their next meal was coming from, Sharon had cut back her schedule and was working only part-time, and her husband had spent virtually his entire career in the not-so-lucrative world of public service. Finally, upon the election of George W. Bush, Sharon's husband had an opportunity to reap the rewards typical in the private sector and commensurate with such a distinguished career. For the first time since they'd been married, the family was finally "pulling down some real coin."

It was probably sometime in 2007 that Sharon had an unsettled feeling when her husband told her that a virtually unknown United States Senator had asked him to co-Chair his Campaign (along with Caroline Kennedy) to be President. She knew that if this candidate won, her husband would very likely be asked to join the new Administration. And if asked, he would serve. And the family would be again living on the salary of a public servant. "Cry Me a River" would be appropriate at this point. Her husband had done very, very well during the eight years that Bush was in office. When asked whether he would accept a position in the Obama administration – presuming Obama won the election and he was asked, Eric replied "Were I to do so, that road leads directly to my wife." But still...

History records that Senator Barack Obama of Illinois was elected President of the United States and Sharon's husband, Eric Holder, was selected as Obama's

Attorney General. The first African-American named to that post.

Obviously, some things have changed for the Holder-Malone household. But Sharon, ever mindful of her humble upbringing, does occasionally have to pinch herself as she goes from a State Dinner to sitting on a porch at the White House and discussing parenting with the First Lady of the United States, Michelle Obama.

Who knew that this child of the deep South – Mobile, Alabama – would one day be in the Oval Office as the President signed a piece of legislation pertaining to Civil Rights? *Who knew* that in her lifetime, the first African-American President would be elected to office and that he would appoint the first African-American Attorney General and that this particular Attorney General would be her husband? *Who knew?*

Steeped in humility, Sharon is in some ways an enigma. At times, she has to pinch herself to be reminded that this woman of a modest upbringing considers the First Lady of the United States among her friends. And yet, at one State Dinner (and it would be very poor form if I were to mention the Prime Minister's name or his country in whose honor the State Dinner was held), Sharon yawned and said to Eric, "Can we go yet?"

Juxtaposed against that episode is a humble, yet refined, woman who is truly grateful for the privilege which she has been fortunate to enjoy. Sharon does carry with her one very large regret: her beloved sister Vivian, who struggled against racism and its injustices for so many years, passed away only three years before being able to witness the election of our nation's first African-American President. And only 63 at her passing, she was far too young to leave this earthly realm.

Chapter 11

A Seminal Event; Finally, an Admission

It was during this period that Doug, Sharon and I were deep in the IBM training program. We were all studying the same training manual when we came upon the word, "vermiculite." Scratching our heads, none of us knew what it meant. And then Sharon chimed in and said, "I think it has something to do with silicon."

I am not proud of the emotions which overcame me at that very instant. My knee-jerk reaction was "...here we go again. She has no more an idea of what vermiculite means than the man in the moon...but she's got to show off." Scouring the office for a dictionary, we found one and quickly turned to the page providing the definition of the word in question. "Vermiculite: a hydrous, silicate mineral." Sharon was correct. <u>She knew something I didn't know</u>. As bizarre as this sounds, it had never happened to me before that a black person knew something that I didn't.

Who knows how and why fate works in the ways it does?

But for me, this seemingly innocuous and mundane event was a seminal moment in the development of my views about race. As trivial as the event was, it was life-altering for me. Almost as though a switch were triggered in my mind, this one event caused me to shift my views about race and to deal with my own racist beliefs. No longer could I claim that I had never met a black person smarter than I. As I was to learn over the course of the decades of our friendship, Sharon isn't smarter than I simply because she could spell "vermiculite." She's simply just smarter. My coming to this conclusion was transformational. And as I met Sharon's friends and family members, I met more and more African-Americans who I would conclude were also smarter than I. The bondage of my racist beliefs had been broken.

IBM, like many companies, large and small, practiced Affirmative Action. But as I was to learn in the IBM "New Manager's Class," generally referred to as "Charm

School," my understanding of Affirmative Action at IBM was incorrect. In Charm School, the question would be posed: "You are evaluating two candidates for the same position. One is black and one is white. Your determination is that they are both equally qualified. Which do you choose?" Virtually the entire class answered that the manager should hire the black candidate. But in IBM's practice of Affirmative Action, that answer was incorrect. The correct answer was to continue to seek out candidates until the hiring manager found one who was, in fact, *more* qualified than any others.

Needless to say, Sharon was not the only black employed by IBM in Atlanta. Several black employees were only a year or less ahead of Doug, Sharon and me. Two of the managers in the office were black. As I got to know them – and I am not proud of these feelings, either – it became clear that none of them could hold a candle to Sharon's intellect, her bearing or her elegance.

In general, the black marketing representatives or systems engineers were part of large teams assigned to significant IBM customers. Consequently, their success or failure was tied to the group's performance and not their individual performance. My view then is no different than it is today. Were these blacks required to "make it on their own," without the benefit of being members of a large team, I think few, if any, would have. But by this point I also was capable of acknowledging that the same was true of many white marketing representatives. They were no different. Had they not been a part of a large team, they too would not have been successful. Success or failure was not a function of race, but of the individual's capabilities – irrespective of the color of their skin.

This was also true of the group that the three of us went through training with. For the most part, it was the same group of "trainees" who met every couple of months in Dallas for a 3-week formal training course. Sharon was obviously popular and the object of desire of many of the black men in our group. And, because these fellows knew that Sharon and I were friends and were from the same branch, I was quite popular: "George, what can you do to get me a date with Sharon?" Of course, I told Sharon about my popularity among this certain group, and she would only chuckle with delight. Once though, a party was being held in one of the apartments. Sharon must have been one of the organizers, because she asked me to have one of her admirers go out and bring some cheese and crackers for the party. Most readers will think that I'm making it up when I say that this gentleman returned with Ritz crackers and Cheese Whiz. And I wish I *were* making it up. But I know that ignorance and perhaps stupidity are not attached to individuals of a certain skin color. It could just as easily been one of the bozo's in our class who were white.

Despite my admittedly "backward" views, if there existed a black woman whose intellect exceeded my own, it was not a great leap for me to believe that there must also be a black man whose intellect surpassed mine. And if he existed, Sharon would undoubtedly cross paths with him. Eric Holder qualifies. People use the expressions "scary-smart" or "wicked-smart" to describe those whose intelligence is not just greater than most, but well above that of most. And so it is with Eric. One doesn't need to spend a lot of time in his presence to realize that he is "scary-smart." "Wicked-smart." The household made up of both Sharon and Eric can only be defined as extraordinary.

I was fortunate to visit Sharon and Eric at their home in the District several years ago. When their son, Buddy, came downstairs I said to him, "Buddy, if you don't know what the word 'vermiculite' means, look it up. It's important." This polite young man could only stare back at me with a look that said "...this friend of mom's has rocks in his head!"

It was on this visit that Sharon warned me before I arrived at their home that I should not be surprised if a Suburban with heavily tinted windows was parked in front of their house. "What's that?" I asked, innocently enough. Sheepishly, Sharon told me that she had her own Secret Service or FBI detail. I introduced myself to the agent before knocking on the front door of the

Holder-Malone house. The agent, who I will identify only by her first name, Susan, was a veteran of the protective service, and while still young, was approaching retirement. And she absolutely adored Sharon – so we had something in common! I wasn't a bit surprised. Sharon is a woman who would treat her protective detail with the same courtesy she would demonstrate to the Chairperson of a Congressional Committee.

During that visit, Sharon had "adopted" a project. Doug Blackmon, a Bureau Chief for the Wall Street Journal had won the Pulitzer Prize for his book, "Slavery by Another Name." The book is an historical account of how slavery persisted well after the signing of the Emancipation Proclamation. Indeed, it endured until the 1940's, although its form was not as overt as the slavery which existed before 1865. Sharon had become Blackmon's "new best friend" and promoted his book with a zeal greater than any huckster at a county fair.

A film was made that was based on the book and debuted at the Sundance Film Festival. And all the while, Sharon was arranging book readings and other events to ensure that Blackmon's book was not overlooked.

On one visit to Washington, D.C., Sharon asked me if I could join her at a book reading that Blackmon was to have at the MLK Library. Of course, I made time to be there. Wandering around this giant public library, I noticed several familiar faces. Sharon didn't know that I have been a political "junkie" all my life and that I wish more than anything that I could trade places with her – or at least shadow her or her distinguished husband. But Sharon had not yet arrived, and I recognized Bill Cohen, the former Senator from Maine and past Secretary of Defense. I also recognized John Lewis, a legend of the Civil Rights Movement who is a sitting Member of the House of Representatives from Georgia. And there were others.

What I didn't realize was that this assemblage, all of us, were awaiting the arrival of a certain Dr. Sharon Malone before beginning the event. Her Secret Service Agent drove the Suburban onto the sidewalk in front of this historic library, and – as spry as a pixie – Dr. Malone hastily made her way to the front of the room. Seeing me – and I must have appeared to be lost – Sharon said simply, "George, have you met my friends?" To which my reply was, "Gosh, Sharon, I don't know who among this crowd are your friends!" She politely introduced me to "Bill," whom I addressed as "Mr. Secretary." And "John," whom I addressed as "Congressman." I shook hands with this living legend of the Civil Rights Movement who had marched arm-in-arm with Dr. Martin Luther King in the early '60's. And then, with no fanfare, we all sat down and listened to Blackmon read a few chapters from his award-winning book.

After Blackmon had completed his reading, a crowd naturally gathered around him to have their copies of his book autographed. Pushing her way to the front, Sharon said, "Doug, this is the friend I told you about. George and I have been friends for over thirty years!" Blackmon politely shook my hand and reached into a space in the podium which held a copy of his book. He handed it to me and thanked me for coming. Flipping through the pages, I noticed that Blackmon had already inscribed a dedication to me. It said simply, "George, it is said that we're known by the company we keep. If you keep company with Sharon, you must be a special guy."

I was at once emotionally moved, spinning in the reflected glory of politicians whom I had only seen on "Meet the Press," and frankly, overwhelmed by the experience. I gave Sharon a kiss good-bye and said that I was going to head back to my hotel. Her agent, Susan, courteously asked if she could give me a ride. And while the thrill of being driven through the District by a Secret Service Agent in a Suburban with blue lights flashing did have a certain appeal, I chose to enjoy the night air as I walked back to my hotel, reflecting on this once-in-a-lifetime experience.

Chapter 12

My Continuing Education

It was possible for a black person to be smarter than I. To know more than I. And my friend Sharon was only the first of many blacks that I would learn were smarter than I and who knew more than I. I was humbled. But it was a humility that I welcomed with open arms.

For over thirty years, Sharon has educated me. When I would make such inane comments as "I have a friend who's black," she would gently correct me. When I said, "I had a roommate who was black," she would say "What color is he now?" Like an idiot, I once said "...black babies are so cute..." Sharon asked me if I didn't think white babies were just as cute.

I was guilty of more than my share of such foibles. While I never considered myself to be particularly "backward," being in Sharon's company somehow could make me appear to be.

And once, upon moving to a particularly "white-bread" neighborhood in Atlanta, I decided that I didn't want the only African-Americans to which my children were exposed to be the men who operated the garbage trucks. Feeling rather self-righteous, I called Sharon and asked her if she could recommend a black pediatrician in my area. Sharon, in her calm manner, said simply, "George, we're going to pretend that you didn't just ask me that. You're going to hang up the phone now, call me back, and ask me if I know of any *good* pediatricians in your area." And so it goes. I am the pupil. Sharon is the teacher. And my thirst for learning more from her is unquenchable.

I can say now that I've met many black people about whom I can say that their intelligence exceeds my own. While this may not seem like much, for this "Hick from Florida's Panhandle," it's saying a lot. But then again, I had an exceptional teacher.

About the Author

When I tell people that I grew up in the "deep south," their next question is "...really, where?" After I answer with "Florida," a series of quizzical stares is predictably followed with a "Really? Florida? Hmmm."

To the casual student of geography – or more particularly of Southern geography – the notion that Florida is in the "Deep South" is often something with which many people take exception. Alabama. Mississippi. Louisiana. Kentucky. Georgia. No question. These states are clearly in the "deep south." But Florida? It's for this reason that in another part of this book I go to considerable lengths explaining that Florida is really two states – and some might even say *three* states. But for anyone who has actually visited hamlets in Florida such as Pea Ridge, Sopchoppy or Two Egg, they will attest that Florida is, indeed, part of what's known generally as the "deep south."

Florida's Panhandle, where our family settled after my father's retirement from the Marine Corps, definitely qualifies as being part of the "deep south." And it may naturally lead someone to ask, "What qualifies a state, a county, a city, a town, a hamlet, a village or, for that matter, a wide spot in the road – to be a part of such an august 'club' as the Deep South?"

Sadly, membership in this club is actually considered by many to be not very desirable. I confess that the criteria which I use to determine or to ascertain membership are entirely subjective. By way of example, if the community in which one lives has a high percentage of its homes domiciled in trailer parks, it is highly probable that he or she is now in the "Deep South."

If one notices that the majority of "those cute little dogs" which may form a "pack" and -- in a fraction of an instant -- surround the observer(s) with teeth bared in a manner which is quite threatening are, quite likely to be a terrier commonly known as a "pit bull" and the observer is quite likely in the "Deep South."

And curiously, and again in an unfair generalization, it seems that this breed is as popular with some black folks as it is with the "rednecks" whose trucks are plastered with Confederate flags. A peculiar irony.

I've noted that upon moving to Florida in the seventh grade, I didn't bring with me any beliefs that differences between black people in Florida and black people in Massachusetts even existed.

But it was a relatively brief period after my family's relocation that these views began to fade – to "evolve" – until eventually I did come to believe that blacks in my new home were *very* different from those I'd left behind in Springfield.

It was this conclusion, or belief, or "evolving" opinion which would disturb me.

Controversial though I knew my views were, they did represent my true feelings *at the time* – although my "true feelings" changed often and are what resulted in the cowardice which led to my protecting, for much of my life, this "dirty little secret" that I was, in fact, a racist. And more importantly, how this evolution itself has led to extraordinary personal growth – and has become the very foundation for this book.

Afterword

It was during the "proofing" of one of the many versions of this book that I felt compelled to note something which is likely not apparent to the reader.

The Foreword of this book – which is largely about my father – could have been written in a very different fashion. I could have begun by describing how monumentally difficult it must have been to be brought up as an orphan. It must have been made even more difficult – orders of magnitude more difficult – given that the cause of his becoming an orphan is that his father abandoned him. He left him. Simply walked out of his life – never to return.

While my sisters and I did not have the best of upbringings, ours was a "walk-in-the-park" when compared to that of our father.

And it was against that backdrop that my father enlisted in the U.S. Marine Corps. And he enlisted after only two years had passed since the conclusion of the greatest war in the history of our nation. And by enlisting in the Marines, he was fully aware that he would not serve as a cook, or as a bookkeeper, or in any such "support" role, as honorable as serving in such roles is. Were our nation to engage in another war requiring combat operations, his role would be "up close and personal" with whomever the enemy would be.

And I could have highlighted the gallantry demonstrated by my father, that the injuries he sustained in Vietnam would afflict him for the rest of his life. Some of these were visible: the hearing aid he required after his last combat tour...the thick glasses he required after that tour.

And I am still simply incapable of fully grasping what it must have been like to kill almost twenty enemy soldiers in hand-to-hand combat with no more than a seven-inch dagger as his only weapon. But many of the injuries which he suffered were unseen. While never diagnosed with PTSD, there is very little doubt that it was a mental health disorder from which he suffered. And the only reason that he was never diagnosed with PTSD is because he rarely went to doctors. And the frequency with which he visited mental health professionals . . . is there a measure of frequency less than "never?"

And I could have acknowledged that my father was, by any objective measure, nothing less than a *bona fide* hero.

And yes, he was a drunk for much of his life. But, in what will not be a "news flash" to any reader who knows me very well – the same could be said of his only son.

I might have noted that while I had a largely difficult relationship with my father, this was not always true of his relationships with my sisters and with his grandchildren. For example, I recall that my daughter Ashley's high school sponsored an event to honor the grandparents of the students of her school. Ashley invited my father, and to my great surprise, he attended. And it was not with reluctance that he attended, but with some level of enthusiasm. And Ashley relates that it was *her* grandfather who was the center of much attention.

And some of my sisters made a genuine effort to "get to know" their father. These efforts were, for the most part, after my mother had passed away. And their efforts were returned with comparable efforts by my father. And the result of their efforts and those of my father led to a degree of reconciliation for some of my sisters.

The "theme" of my marriage to Leslie was that of "Reconciliation." Toward that end, I asked my father if he would honor me by serving as my Best Man. He accepted my invitation without hesitation. And during his toast, he said something along the lines of, "Son, you are a good guy and my own father was not such a good guy..." Without any context, many of those who heard the toast were unable to process the significance of it. And yet, in his own way, he was responding to my "olive branch," asking him to serve as my Best Man, with one of his own. Rarely did my father refer to his own father. And so this was an event of some considerable significance – at least to me. And I could have included this and the other, more positive, efforts which he made, but did not.

And no, he didn't come to my Little League games in Springfield. He didn't "play catch" with me. But on those rare occasions – those precious few times – that he would visit my team's baseball practice wearing his "Dress Blues," I could overhear the other boys whispering to each other, "Who is that? I wonder if he has a gun?" During those occasions, my chest would swell with pride: "That's my father. He's a Marine."

And so the whole team would race to my father and surround him – a man who knew virtually nothing about baseball and who cared to learn even less – the team would literally encircle him and ask him to explain *each* of the many medals which adorned his uniform and what he did to be awarded each of them. "Bye-bye, team practice!" My teammates had a new priority. And I could not have been prouder.

I could have acknowledged what an accomplished artist – a potter – my father had become and the many awards he won for his artistic work; work as different from his experience in the Marines as light is from dark.

But I did not make that choice. And the choice I made was one I knew would have consequences – and that these consequences would probably result from the disappointment in me that my sisters likely would have.

My sisters' disappointment with me will result from at least two things: firstly, the Devitt's are private people, and arguably, with good reason. To read, in print, that both of your parents were drunks for most of their lives...well, that's probably not done in most families and it certainly isn't done by Devitt's. And so it was with my eyes wide open that I chose to break a fundamental, though unspoken, rule in our family.

I made a conscious choice to err on the side of transparency . . . of honesty . . . of truth. I had some views about race which were admittedly pretty radical. They were not in the mainstream of society. And my revealing them would, I knew, not be a proud moment. But because my views were so radical, I felt the reader deserved to have as honest a portrayal of my life as possible so that if he or she cared to understand where someone so warped in his thinking came from – what kind of an upbringing could possibly lead to the development of the views which I held – it was incumbent upon me to provide the reader with that capability.

The other reason that my sisters will be disappointed in me derives from the very conscious choice I made of how to portray my father. And as I have acknowledged, it was possible to have portrayed my father in a vastly different, vastly more positive light. I could have chosen the "hero track." And I'd have been "technically" correct in that portrayal. As I've acknowledged, my father was, and always will be, a *bona fide* hero.

Many – perhaps most – of those who know me and who are reading this will be surprised, and a smaller number of those who know me and who are reading this will not be surprised, to learn that I could be portrayed *objectively* as carrying on a life-long battle with my own demons.

Sigmund Freud and Carl Jung, psychoanalysts from the early 20th Century, argued that the father is very important to the boy's development of identity.

In his book *Absent Fathers, Lost Sons,* Guy Corneau writes that *the presence of the father's body during the son's developmental phases is integral in the son developing a positive sense of self as masculine.*

Another news flash for the reader: my father was absent from my life for most of the years which comprised my "early childhood development." He was gone. He didn't come home every night for dinner as most fathers did. And this was not because he *wanted* to be absent, but because he was serving our nation in places like Guantanamo Bay, Cuba, and in South and North Vietnam, as well as in Korea.

And thus, to the degree that the reader subscribes to Freud and Jung's views – or for that matter, subscribes to any of the numerous schools of thought within the various *and* varied psychological communities regarding *Masculine Psychology* or the *Psychology of Male Human Identity* – to not have included as much relevant information about my father as possible would have been intellectually dishonest. To put it more directly: if the reader believes that the relationship between the father and the son in the years associated with Early Childhood Development have any bearing on the son's psyche during the period of his adulthood, it was incumbent upon me to include the information which I did.

But it is for these two reasons that I had to make a choice: would I characterize my father in a way which would provide the reader with some insight into how a grown man of above-average intellect could possibly have arrived at conclusions regarding race which the vast majority of society would – frankly – find repulsive? Or would I choose to characterize my father as the hero which he indeed was?

To have chosen this latter characterization of my father would not have honestly reflected the *significance* of the impact he had upon my life. And so, it was my determination that to choose the "hero" depiction of my father would not be a completely honest reflection of how I became the person that I am.

Lastly, it is my fervent hope…it is, in fact, my prayer, that whatever dysfunctional cycle resulted as a consequence of my father's relationship (or lack of one) with his father and my relationship with my father – that this "cycle" ends with me, with my generation, and that my own son and daughters will indeed be proud of their grandfather – as they *should* be, but that I will not pass on those things which have resulted in many of my own dysfunctions.

My hope is that they will inherit the good. And truly, there is much good. But that I will not continue the cycle of curses which have afflicted virtually every generation of the Devitt family. I will not pass on my emotional dysfunctions, the cycle of abusing alcohol and other substances, the cycle of physical or emotional harm, or both, inflicted on those whom we most love by each of us who carry the name of George Ernest Devitt: whether it is George Ernest Devitt, Sr., George Ernest Devitt, Jr., or George Ernest Devitt III.

And so it is that I *declare* that these unhealthy cycles shall end now, with me. And it is only by God's Grace that this will be possible.

And so I seek His Grace and His Favor. And I ask very specifically that my Savior break this cycle. For good. Forever.

And I know that this is the same Savior who put Sharon Malone in my life. And Sharon has made me a better person just by her presence.

And because my Savior reflects all that is good, all that is right and all that is just, I am wholly confident that He will shower His Grace upon all of the members of my generation of the Devitt family. And the result will be that the generational curses which afflict those of us whose name is Devitt will finally be broken.

I am not just "wholly confident." There is *nothing* about which I could be more certain.

www.ingramcontent.com/pod-product-compliance
Lightning Source LLC
Chambersburg PA
CBHW080338290526
45790CB00010B/3748